The ALCHEMIST'S HANDBOOK

Also by John Randolph Price

(Selected audiocassettes are also available from Hay House)

✳✳✳

The
ALCHEMIST'S
HANDBOOK

John Randolph Price

HAY HOUSE, INC.
Carlsbad, California
London • Sydney • Johannesburg
Vancouver • Hong Kong

Published and distributed in the United States by: Hay House, Inc., P.O. Box 5100, Carlsbad, CA 92018-5100 • *Phone:* (760) 431-7695 or (800) 654-5126 • *Fax:* (760) 431-6948 or (800) 650-5115 • www.hayhouse.com • *Published and distributed in Australia by:* Hay House Australia Pty. Ltd., 18/36 Ralph St., Alexandria NSW 2015 • *Phone:* 612-9669-4299 • *Fax:* 612-9669-4144 • www.hayhouse.com.au • *Published and distributed in the United Kingdom by:* Hay House UK, Ltd. • Unit 62, Canalot Studios • 222 Kensal Rd., London W10 5BN • *Phone:* 44-20-8962-1230 • *Fax:* 44-20-8962-1239 • www.hayhouse.co.uk • *Published and distributed in the Republic of South Africa by:* Hay House SA (Pty), Ltd., P.O. Box 990, Witkoppen 2068 • *Phone/Fax:* 2711-7012233 • orders@psdprom.co.za • *Distributed in Canada by:* Raincoast • 9050 Shaughnessy St., Vancouver, B.C. V6P 6E5 • *Phone:* (604) 323-7100 • *Fax:* (604) 323-2600

Editorial supervision: Jill Kramer • *Design: Summer McStravick*

The author of this book does not dispense medical advice or prescribe the use of any technique as a form of treatment for physical or medical problems without the advice of a physician, either directly or indirectly. The intent of the author is only to offer information of a general nature to help you in your quest for emotional and spiritual well-being. In the event you use any of the information in this book for yourself, which is your constitutional right, the author and the publisher assume no responsibility for your actions.

Library of Congress Cataloging-in-Publication Data

Price, John Randolph.
    The alchemist's handbook / John Randolph Price.
       p. cm.
    Includes bibliographical references.
    ISBN 1-56170-747-3
    1. Spiritual life--Miscellanea. 2. Alchemy--Religious aspects--Miscellanea. I. Title.

BF1999 .P717 2000
299'.93--dc21
                                        00-038883

ISBN 13: 978-1-56170-747-8
ISBN 10: 1-56170-747-3

07 06 05 04   7 6 5 4
1st printing, August 2000
4th printing, December 2004

Printed in Canada

Dedicated

to the

New Alchemists

Contents

Introduction

$\mathcal{M}$ost writers of spiritual books are continually seeking new ideas to express the eternal truths of being, and to help their readers (and themselves) realize their innate divinity and achieve mastery over this world. In the process, parallels in New Physics and Ageless Wisdom have been documented, psychology and metaphysics have been interwoven, Jesus' teachings have been reinterpreted in line with new revelations, and philosophic mysteries have been brought into the light for greater understanding of those ancient treasures.

Yet, I have said to myself many times that there must still be exciting new ways to make practical applications of the old secret formulas—different courses of action to rapidly accelerate the realization of peace and plenty, and dissolve the false belief that conflict and scarcity could possibly exist in a universe of love and infinite givingness. This silent decree was obviously picked up by my wife, Jan, who announced to me in the fall of 1998 that we should schedule a special Intensive on the subject of *alchemy*. She said, "The thought just came to me."

That thought led to research on the principles of this ancient science—particularly the classification called *dynamic alchemy*, which dealt with mental vibrations to create a Perfect World, and not the changing of lead into gold. I soon realized that this method of fulfilling material needs and desires might not be readily accepted by those who did not believe that the material world is in unity with the spiritual, or that God is fully present and active in the affairs of everyone living on the physical plane. But these are alchemical truths—that God is omnipresent and fully manifest in both the invisible and visible worlds.

Dynamic alchemy calls for us to fully understand cause and effect, mind and manifestation, energy and matter, and to move from what may be considered passive spirituality to positive assertiveness in our rediscovery of the ideal life.

To continue, we studied ancient texts; the teachings of the secret societies of the Middle Ages; and the references to mythology, planetary energies, and the mysteries of all ages. (Dynamic alchemy acknowledges the *inclusiveness* of all symbolic philosophy.) We found that this science is veiled in mystery and highly esoteric, and must be properly interpreted for today's matter-of-fact world. For example, an alchemist might say:

> *The Eternal Present impregnates the Veiled Virgin to unveil the Mater . . . the Dance of Shiva plants the seed of fulfillment; the Mother births the objective reality.*

In decoding the message, we would see that *The Eternal Present* is another term for "Saturn," the Energy of Success and Fulfillment. The *Veiled Virgin* is "Isis," the Energy of Union and Receptivity (also referred to as *Creative Wisdom* in my angel books); while the *Mater* is the "Energy of Isis and Venus" (Power of Abundance) combined as the World Mother.

The *Dance of Shiva* is another reference to Saturn. What this means is that as illumined consciousness impresses the Feminine Principle within, the enhanced feeling nature becomes the birthing mechanism for form and experience in the outer world.

We also perused metaphysical literature dealing with the *alchemy of mind*, including previous books I had written, and combined this outer work with daily meditation for greater understanding of the process. Next, we applied the principles to make specific changes in our lives, and fully satisfied with the value of the teaching and the validity of the science, we announced an Intensive, sponsored by The Quartus Foundation, to be held in the spring.

On March 4, 1999, 30 people from the U.S. and abroad gathered at the Tapatio Springs Resort in Boerne, Texas, to commence a three-day school on the Science of Alchemy. We studied, meditated, questioned, exchanged views, and as a group, wove the ancient links of the alchemical chain into a mighty power, which, as you will see, brought forth extraordinary manifestations—some considered truly miraculous.

This book is based on the principles taught at the school, with new material added to make it a more comprehensive, yet easy-to-understand work on the process of dynamic alchemy. Specific attention is placed on the material world as an extension of mind rather than an illusion, and a step-by-step procedure is given to bring into visibility the forms and experiences you choose for greater joy and fulfillment in life.

To again clarify the position that this process takes in creating a new world, dynamic alchemy strongly focuses on our personal identity as an expression of Spirit, and emphasizes the mind as *spiritual* power, a creative force—not a "mortal" nonpower. Regarding the latter part, if we think of our mind as independent of God, we are reinforcing the belief in separation.

And to deny the mind's creative power can reduce a person to utter helplessness. As *A Course in Miracles* so beautifully states it, "Few appreciate the real power of the mind, and no one remains fully aware of it all the time. . . . The mind is very powerful, and never loses its creative force. . . . It is hard to recognize that thought and belief combine into a power surge that can literally move mountains."[1]

Kenneth Wapnick, a clinical psychologist who teaches on the *Course,* writes: "The only true cause in this world is the mind . . . and all aspects of the material world are the mind's effect. There can be no exceptions to this principle, for the mind is the only creative agent."[2] *Agent* is a key word here, meaning "representative"—a creative "intermediary" between the invisible and visible forces.

Is this leaving God out of the equation? Certainly not. The activity of God is the manifesting energy that produces the effect according to what the mind chooses, decrees, and believes. And when our minds are identified with the Divine thought system of our Essential Self, that which is manifest is love fulfilled on earth as it is in heaven.

By recognizing the power of the mind and the unity of spirit and matter, dynamic alchemy progresses from spiritual mysticism to *Divine Materialism*—Creative Principle at work *materializing* in the world of form—which is, as I point out later, "wholly sanctioned by the Great Power ordering all things, and the Great Thought producing all things." It is a spiritual process for those who are ready to assume responsibility for their lives as active *co-creators*. When we recognize our true identity and focus our minds in and as Spirit, we realize that abundance and scarcity, success and failure, health and sickness, and harmony and conflict cannot coexist. We change our minds, choose the highest in life, and let the other fade into the nothingness from which it came. And that which is manifest in the phenomenal world comes forth as an expression of Divine Grace, the infinite givingness of God.

Sai Baba, the Indian holy man, avatar, and most definitely a master alchemist, says: "For accomplishing any objective, two things are needed: individual effort and Divine Grace. The two are like the negative and positive poles of a magnet. If there is only Divine Grace, but no proper effort on the part of the individual, the object cannot be achieved."[3] Through the alchemical process (individual effort), we condition consciousness to literally become the Shining Sun of Grace.

This book veers away from the accepted idea of conscious and subconscious mind and underscores the fact that while we are not all of God, God is all of us, including the mind of decision and choice and the principle of creative power. It also borrows heavily from mythology, those dimensions of mystery uniting heaven and earth—the messages of truth brought forth from ancient times. And, I emphasize the reality and great importance of the inner archetypes as symbolized by the Tarot—the Living Energies within that were revealed thousands of years ago in ancient Egypt as aspects of God that sustain our personal realities. We will be working closely with these mighty spiritual forces as intermediaries between the invisible and visible worlds.

In addition, I delve into the astrological energies, the universal Grand Design. The alchemical view is that nothing beneficial and of value exists that was not created by God. The planetary energies do indeed exist as forces of God, and their divine influence is to help us understand our potentials and tendencies, and indicate the trend of outer life circumstances.

As Ralph Waldo Emerson said, "The way to mend the bad world is to create the right world." That is what we're doing with dynamic alchemy, creating our ideal world. And quoting

Emerson again, "The only sin is limitation" and "we are the builders of our fortunes"—so be prepared to enter into a new experience of recognizing and using your extraordinary powers, forgiving your limitations, and of building a life filled with good fortune.

Dynamic alchemy will be a course of personal creative action that will yield rich dividends in life as the principles are understood and practiced. May all your hopes, wishes, and dreams be realized.

❋❋❋

Chapter One

Dynamic Alchemy

*T*he science of alchemy demonstrates that the laws of the spiritual and material world are one and the same. It is the science of the Masters of Wisdom that brings forth the fulfillment of material needs in cooperation with spiritual understanding.

There are two basic classifications of alchemy:

1. Mundane alchemy, the taking of a base metal, purifying it, then introducing minute quantities of other compounds to liberate the energy and produce a new property, usually gold. Manly P. Hall, the renowned philosophical researcher, has written that "the Chaldeans, Phoenicians, and Babylonians were familiar with the principles of alchemy, as were many early Oriental races. . . . According to the fragmentary writings of those early peoples, alchemy was to them no speculative art."[1] This form of alchemy reached its high point in the 1400s.

2. Dynamic alchemy (from Greek *dynamikos*, relating to energy in motion; originally called "Divine" alchemy). This is the recognition of the unity of spirit and matter, and through certain techniques, it reverses the polarity of one's physical life on the material plane from a lower vibration to the desired quality.

The earlier science of Divine alchemy began in ancient Egypt and was discovered by Hermes Trismegistus, the father of occult wisdom. The teachings of Hermes "really constituted the basic principles of 'The Art of Hermetic Alchemy,' which, contrary to general belief, dealt in the mastery of Mental Forces, rather than Material Elements—the Transmutation of one kind of Mental Vibrations into others, instead of changing of one kind of metal into another. The legends of the 'Philosopher's Stone,' which would turn base metal into Gold, was an allegory relating to Hermetic Philosophy, readily understood by all students of true Hermeticism."[2]

It is believed that Moses was also a master alchemist, and borrowing from the teachings of Hermes, he brought forth the secret doctrine of Israel. *Moses* was an ancient name for "the sun," a symbol of alchemy. An Egyptian, Moses was initiated in the Egyptian Mysteries, and later established a secret school for the Israelites called the Tabernacle Mysteries. The essence of the teachings was that all things were of one life and substance—that individual being is not all of God, but God is all of individual being. Through the same power that created the universe, a person can create his or her perfect world.

After the word *energy* was conceived in the 300s B.C., the alchemical process—following basically the same axioms—became more secularized in order to remove it from "religious" orientation. Spiritual, yes, but not related to church-religion. *Dynamic* alchemy as the force and power of manifestation was then taught in the Greek Mystery Schools, and later in the Sacred Academy in Alexandria, Egypt.

Dynamic Alchemy continued to flourish in secret societies, and was said to be the basic doctrine of such notables as

Roger Bacon, Paracelsus, St. Germain, Leonardo da Vinci, Isaac Newton, Victor Hugo, and Claude Debussy—all dedicated alchemists who used the power of their minds to reveal the highest reality on the physical side of life. Debussy, for example, wrote music to unite taste, touch, sight, and sound—the sensations of the material world.

Although we are not of this world, let's remember that we're definitely in it as far as our physical incarnation is concerned at this point in our eternal lives. We are here to live fully—as complete beings—for the joy of it. Sadness and sorrow, conflict and chaos, are not a part of our divine inheritance.

But dynamic alchemy—a form of *Divine Materialism* and wholly sanctioned by the Great Power ordering all things and the Great Thought producing all things—began fading out in the mid-1800s. It happened with the introduction of a teaching with the stated purpose of proving that there was no reality in matter—that the objective world was only an illusion—and the doctrine quickly spread in metaphysical circles.

It is true that an effect is only temporary in time and space, yet it is the symbol of the energy pattern, the changeless reality of God, out of which the form or thing becomes visible. And let's remember that regardless of the element of impermanence, spiritual supply manifest as form or experience in "this world" is certainly real.

To continue this further, if nothing really exists, why bother with life? The denial of the reality of this world severely inhibits all natural urges to express, for if there is the belief that there is no true objective world, the energies of mind turn back on self in repression. And when the creative power of individual being (and the true teachings of Jesus) are not recognized, all passion for living fades away. Let's agree that the only "illusion" of this world is the belief that we are less than divine; and the false images of scarcity, futility, and debilitation that arise from this belief and are projected on the screen of life.

Ageless wisdom tells us that dynamic alchemy was the essential force in bringing about a true spiritual transmutation in an individual. And the reason is that when we truly understand the law of cause and effect and the unity of energy and matter, the spiritual awakening is greatly accelerated. Think of it this way: The life of the seeker of truth can be bliss without harvest, yet when one understands the principles of dynamic alchemy, there is *fruitful* ecstasy.

The dynamic alchemists believed in the essential unity of the Cosmos. As an ancient teaching tells us, "Matter is spirit at its lowest point of manifestation, and spirit is matter at its highest." It was also taught that spirit and matter are equal because all is God, not as a reflection of God, but God as everything in the physical universe. Later, Spinoza, the great Dutch philosopher, said that mind and matter are the same thing. And Emerson was strong in his conviction that the material world is an expression of a spiritual system—that the visible and invisible were united as one and governed by spiritual laws. Then came Einstein with the revelation that energy and mass are equal, identical, and interchangeable. With the realization of the parallel nature of science and philosophy, dynamic alchemy (couched primarily in psychological terms at this point) began to reappear, with its basic principles embraced by certain segments of the New Thought Movement.

The alchemists have always known that there is a correspondence or analogy existing between things spiritual and things physical, the same laws operating in each realm. As the alchemical axiom in the *Kybalion* (ancient compilations of basic Hermetic Doctrines) states it: *"As above, so below; as below, so above."* This is the Principle of Correspondence and is a Universal Law. "The ancient Hermetists considered this Principle as one of the most important mental instruments by which man was able to pry aside the obstacles which hid from view the Unknown."[3] And it was written that through this understanding, Noah built the ark, Moses built his tabernacle, and Solomon his temple, which brings us to this definition:

Dynamic alchemy is the science of bringing about a visible form, condition, or experience by building an idealized structure in mind together with an understanding of (1) the Alchemical Sun of God, (2) the Spiritual Forces, (3) the Penetrating Law, (4) the Receptive Sheath, and (5) the emanation of the World Mother.

Professional researcher and author Barbara G. Walker has written: "As a system of mysticism, alchemy was permeated by sexual symbols. So-called 'copulations' and 'marriages' figured in alchemical procedures. Sexual drawings enlivened the texts. The Alchemical Rebus was the usual bisexual image of male and female powers in union . . ."[4]

You will see examples of this in the third and fourth alchemical steps as one phase of soul enters into a sexual affinity with another to "birth" the desired form or experience.

At this point, we may think of Jesus' instruction to "not be anxious about your life" but to "seek first his kingdom and his righteousness, and all these things shall be yours as well." What is the kingdom? The alchemists said it was the Perfect World, the domain within individual consciousness where everything spiritual *and* material already exists as thought-forms, as symbolized by the sun in the sky and gold in the earth. The Son or True Self (Sun) sees the material form (gold) as fully manifest—not to come but existing as a present reality. To seek first the kingdom means to focus your attention on that which is already yours—a perfect world both spiritually *and* materially, seen first through the inner vision, and then through the physical eyes as it is brought forth into materialization.

Before we proceed with the specific steps in dynamic alchemy and discuss the links in the manifestation chain, I want you to think about the answer to this question: *What kind of life in this physical-material world do I really want?* Ponder this for several minutes before moving to the next chapter.

❋❋❋

Chapter Two

See the
Ultimate in Life

*Y*ou are a spiritual being in a physical form living in a material universe over a span of years. Now think: How do you want to live? What do you want to have, to be, and to do? Think *materially*. What kind of life can you see for yourself? Think *physically*.

Can you see yourself living with lavish sums of money? Don't say that money is not spiritual, isn't important to you, or that you are not worthy enough to be wealthy. The great metaphysical alchemist W. Frederic Keeler has written:

> To question whether you deserve money, or whether it is right to have it, is to deny it to YOURSELF. No such attitude has to do with adjustment. The world reads your doubt and transforms it into lack. You are a master. Scorn money and it will leave you, for that scorn is at such a time, your base but royal decree. A dog will not abide scorn. Friends flee from it. Wall Street will tell you that money is very sensitive. All things are intelligent. Therefore all things obey

intelligence. . . . Dollars will not even nod to you as they pass you by.[1]

Don't feel guilty about wanting money. It is a manifestation of spirit, and you are deserving of an all-sufficiency of spirit-in-form.

Can you see yourself as wonderfully successful in your chosen career, or in your creative activities regardless of your age? What do you really want to do for the rest of your life? Reach for the stars and capture your highest vision. If you can't find the right picture in mind of true success for you, find a symbol or symbolic gesture. When I first began the alchemical program, my symbol of success was me standing on the top of a mountain, arms outstretched, and saying, "Thank you, God" with deep feelings of gratitude. That soon led to strong mental images of what I wanted to achieve in this lifetime.

Look at the people in your life. Is your vision one of loving, harmonious relationships with everyone? In your perfect world, why on earth would you want to feel resentment or ill will toward anyone? Wouldn't it be ideal to be friends with all the world and have all the world be friends with you? And if there's not the perfect love-mate in your life—and you desire such a relationship—why not do what's necessary on the inner planes to establish the magnetic attraction? As Anthony Hopkins's character says to Brad Pitt's in the movie *Meet Joe Black:* "Love is passion . . . to make the journey and not fall deeply in love, you haven't lived a life at all. But you have to try, because if you haven't tried, you haven't lived."

How do you feel about your physical body? Is it whole, strong, vital, and in a state of well-being? The energy and power of the alchemical process does not understand any such word as *sick* or *disease*. It sees only perfection as the natural order of things. Are you willing to be well and strong so that you may live life to the fullest without concern for health?

Look at your clothes, your transportation, and all that you consider worthwhile in your world of possessions. Does everything rank in the category of ultimate satisfaction and contentment? What about your dwelling place, the furnishings in each room, the table you set, and the art on the walls? As you move through your home, is there true beauty? "The Mysteries held that man, in part at least, was the product of his environment. Therefore, they considered it imperative that every person be surrounded by objects which would evoke the highest and noblest sentiments. They proved that it was possible to produce beauty in life by surrounding life with beauty."[2]

You have the opportunity now to structure your life according to your highest ideals—your greatest hopes, wishes, and dreams. Open your journal and begin to write what would make you happiest in life. Don't hold back. Paint a masterpiece with words, and then before you finish this book, be prepared to change it as your imagination stretches to see an even greater and grander life.

Once you know beyond a shadow of a doubt that nothing is too good for you, that you are worthy of a royal life of beauty and nobility—*with all things added*—you will become a master alchemist. And with that ability, you will help others to realize their full potential in life. Perhaps that is why you have come into incarnation at this time.

❋❋❋

Chapter Three

The Alchemical Sun

*N*ow we begin to forge the links in the alchemical process, first by understanding the truth that God is all of individual being.

The dynamic alchemists believed that Father-Power activated the Mother-Substance inherent in the one infinite Presence to produce a universal field of Solar Energy, which expressed individually as Suns of God. *Sun* is the proper alchemical term, rather than "son," as it refers to Solar (Soul) energy. Also, an individual's energy field resembles the fiery, vibrant, pulsating, shining sun in the sky. To the alchemists, *our God is an all-consuming fire*, a Universal Consciousness that *particularizes* as individual consciousness, as the Light of the world, as the radiating energy of manifestation.

I and God are one. God is all I am. All that God has is mine. What do I, you, have? Everything for a life of total fulfillment. The Universal Consciousness of Wholeness, Abundance, Success, and Harmony individualizes as the Kingdom of All-That-Is. Think, know . . . *God so loved the Sun that a world* crowned with ecstasy was given, the fullness of life assured. Nothing is missing. We are the Identity of Self-completion.

Say to yourself:

I feel my Self as the Spiritual Fire of God.
I see my Self as an auric field of Divine Fire.
I know my Self as a Holy Sun of God.

I am the Shining Sun of Life.
I am the Shining Sun of Love.
I am the Shining Sun of Infinite Supply.

Our true and only Self is God Immanent, the Master Mind that constitutes the reality of our being. Drill yourself in the Truth that you are the universal Spirit of God manifest *as* you. You are the fullness of the Godhead Selfing Itself as the mighty Sun and flowing forth to create a Perfect World.

Think on these thoughts adapted from my book *The Jesus Code*[1]:

God IS. God is the one universal Presence and Power, the Cosmic Heart of Love, expressing as all that is good, true, and beautiful in life. I am that Expression.

I and the Spirit of God are one and the same. I am God being me, and God loves Itself as me.

I am now aware of the I mighty in the midst of me, my one Self expressing as perfect life and perfect world.

I renounce the false belief that I am a human being and accept the truth that I am pure Spirit. God is my only Being, my only Existence.

*I am not a human mind, for there is only one
Mind, God-Mind, and God did not create anything
opposite of Itself.*

*I am conscious of my only Self, the Truth of my
Being. I am aware of Me, the only One, and through
this awareness of my Self, the kingdom flows into
perfect form and experience.*

To be a successful alchemist, you must assume this Divine
Identity and work only from love—the love of your whole Self
and everyone else as that Self. Dynamic alchemy is not greedy
or selfish; it is for the good of all, and what you want for yourself, you must want for all. This is what love is all about.

Say to yourself:

*I love everyone without exception. As I think
about the past and present, my mind may focus on
certain individuals who evoke less-than-desirable
emotions in me. I now transmute that negative
energy by forgiving them and speaking words of
unconditional love.*

*[Speak the name aloud] . . . I love you. I love you
unconditionally. I love you for Who and What you
are, with no strings attached. I am love. You are love.
We are one in love, and we are healed through love.*

*I now bring into my consciousness my home and
family, my place of work, my city, state, and country,
my world—and I send forth love to heal and harmonize every negative condition on this planet. I feel
the love pouring forth from my heart center, and I
know that this Love Power will accomplish that for
which it is sent. I am love in action!*

Now think on these thoughts:

May everyone in the world be well.
May everyone in the world be rich.
May everyone in the world be successful.
May everyone in the world be loved and loving.

As an alchemical exercise—in preparation for the master process later—focus on the Universal Spirit individualizing as you. See with the mind's eye, and feel in the depths of your heart the dynamics of the whole fiery Universe condensing itself and becoming a brilliant Shining Sun. This is your particular energy field, the Life Force called *you*. Now see-feel the light flowing out from the Sun you are as the creative power of manifestation.

As you do this, say to yourself:

I am the Universal Consciousness of Wholeness individualized and in radiant expression.
I am the Universal Consciousness of Abundance individualized and in radiant expression.
I am the Universal Consciousness of Success individualized and in radiant expression.
I am the Universal Consciousness of Right Relations individualized and in radiant expression.

Practice this exercise until the abstract imaging and the thoughts of truth are together as one. You will see the importance of this later.

✳✳✳

Chapter Four

The Spiritual Forces

*T*hese spiritual forces are the 22 Causal Powers that I wrote about in my book *The Angels Within Us:*

The universe is a macrocosm of creative energy and power, and every man, woman, and child is the epitome of this totality of the cosmos. Within your individualized energy field, the microcosm called you, are 22 Causal Powers, or angels, that control your conscious behavior and govern the manifestation of all forms and experiences in your personal life. Their existence has been taught since the beginning of spiritual brotherhoods and philosophical societies thousands of years ago. In ancient Egypt, the 22 Powers were shown as hieroglyphs representing the laws of all phenomena, and one of the volumes saved from the burning library of Alexandria contained detailed descriptions of these angels.

These are the living Governors of Life, each controlling a Gate, or opening, leading to the phenomenal world—conditioning and determining all outer expression.[1]

The Powers live on the inner planes of consciousness as Archetypes, Living Energies, extensions of our Whole Self, and are pictured symbolically as the 22 major trumps of the Tarot.

We will soon be focusing on four of these Archetypes in our alchemy work—with the blending and activity of an additional one later in the process. (The number 5 is the ancient symbol of individual being.) Our objective is to make sure that at the onset, all 22 are in harmony with each other and with the personality. Because of ego projections, there may be some imbalance in their energies, and we do not want any vibrational interference internally.

For those of you who have read *The Angels Within Us,* or its sequel, *Angel Energy,* you know how to move into inner space for a meeting. For others, simply consent to the truth that these whirlpools of power exist within you. Then go into meditation and contemplate these energies of Spirit as ministering angels, hands of God, that are given to help you on your journey through life. Next, ask your guardian angel or Inner Guide to come forth and take you to meet them. The Inner Guide is an aspect of Spirit that is very helpful in escorting you to higher realms of consciousness during meditation. It is a form of energy that may take on the shape of a "human" male figure to accompany you through the inner maze to the realm of the archetypes.

For our purpose now, you will want to talk to all 22 at the same time in the "Council Room" on the inner plane. Feel the Inner Guide's hand in yours and the love, wisdom, and power enfolding you as you walk through what seems to be a winding tunnel. At a certain point, you will see lights ahead, and beings with form and appearance will come into your imaging faculty. It is all right to use your imagination at first to mentally picture the shape and form of these Causal Powers, but they will quickly show you an appearance on the screen of your mind.

In a few cases, their names will vary from the ones I used in my angel books, as I refer here to their basic alchemical functions. For example, although it is the same energy, Isis—the Angel of Creative Wisdom—is now called the Angel of Union and Receptivity, and later you will understand why. For reference, I show the original angel names in parentheses.

The archetypes are:

The Angel of Unconditional Love and Freedom
The Angel of Creative Intelligence (Angel of Illusion and Reality)
The Angel of Union and Receptivity (Angel of Creative Wisdom)
The Angel of Abundance
The Angel of Power and Authority
The Angel of Spiritual Understanding
The Angel of Loving Relationships
The Angel of Victory and Triumph
The Angel of Order and Harmony
The Angel of Discernment
The Angel of Expansion and Good Fortune (Angel of Cycles and Solutions)
The Angel of Spiritual Strength and Will
The Angel of Renunciation and Regeneration
The Angel of Spiritual Rebirth (Angel of Death and Rebirth)
The Angel of Patience and Acceptance
The Angel of Materiality and Temptation
The Angel of Courage and Perseverance
The Angel of Service and Synthesis
The Angel of Imagination and Liberation
The Angel of Truth and Enlightenment
The Angel of the Creative Word
The Angel of Success and Fulfillment (Angel of Success)

Once you have a visual impression or a feeling of their presence, address the group with these words:

*I have called this meeting with pure intentions
and love in my heart. I am embarking on a dynamic
alchemical process to change my life from a lower
vibration to the highest ideal, and I need your full
cooperation. I ask you to balance your masculine
and feminine qualities, to harmonize any conflicting
energy patterns, and to work together as a team in
full support of the new polarity. To do this, let us
meditate together on love, joy, and peace.*

We are the love of God as one. (Pause for a moment in the silence.) *We are the joy of God as one.*
(Silence.) *We are the peace of God as one.* (Silence.)
*Our vibrations are now in harmony, and divine
order prevails throughout the inner planes of
consciousness.*

Now listen for any response from within. An angel may have something to say regarding a personality characteristic that should be brought under control, or offer other helpful advice to remove an ego projection. Listen, and write what you receive in your journal.

Your next activity in the contact with these Living Energies is to ensure that the Angel of Power and Authority and the Angel of Spiritual Strength and Will are bonded together and working as one in your consciousness. The objective is to fuse the energies of these two powers into one force that will condition the personal sense (personality) in preparation for the receiving of the energy of the Angel of Success and Fulfillment, Saturn, the great Law of Cause and Effect. We will work with the Master Light of Saturn in the next two chapters, but for now, let's look at the function and divine intentions of these two angels.

The Angel of Power and Authority

This angel within was called Osiris by the Egyptians. He was the brother-husband of Isis, and represents the material aspect of the sun, which vitalizes the earth. It is the Emperor of the Tarot, symbolizing power, authority, and self-control. Astrologically, this angel is represented by Aries, the *power-to-be*, and his positive attributes are vigor, vitality, and strong decisiveness, with reliance on the Will of God. This holy helper strengthens the will to serve the divine plan and provides the power to carry you over the obstacles of life.

The Angel of Spiritual Strength and Will

This particular energy has been called the Daughter of the Flaming Sword, implying a feminine quality. However, it is a synthesis of both feminine and masculine energies, since the aspects of strength and will are perfectly blended into one power or force. The young woman in the Tarot represents spiritual strength, and the picture shows her hands on the mouth of a lion. This energy is represented by Leo in astrology, providing the aspirant will, enthusiasm, inspiration, confidence, and vitality. She also works in consciousness to tame the lion of aggression, overconfidence, and self-satisfaction.

In your meditative state, call these two angels to you. The Angel of Power and Authority will appear as the fiery figure of a powerful man, while the Angel of Spiritual Strength and Will may show herself as a young woman with a pulsating light body. Ask them to blend their energies, and in that oneness, to be the initial causal powers to engage the personality and prepare your consciousness for the later infusion of the Saturn energy. They will understand the meaning of your request and the importance of the fusion.

Now see their energy forms coming together as one Being of Light and moving into the forefront of your consciousness—of your mental and feeling natures. Know and feel the embodiment of these powerful energies. Know and feel the new initiative, the power and vitality of I AM. Know and feel the strength and determination of I WILL. Say to yourself:

> *My life is ruled only by spiritual power, embodying the fullness of God's Purpose and Power. I am leaving ego domination and rising into the reality of spiritual consciousness.*
>
> *I am strong in the mightiness of Spirit, and I am undaunted. My mind is firmly one-pointed in seeing only the good. My heart is fearless and knows only the emotion of victory.*

You will repeat these steps when we begin the alchemical process. Until that time, practice *being* the Power-to-Be and the Will-for-Good. Know your purpose and power. Feel your strength and will.

✳✳✳

Chapter Five

Saturn:
The Penetrating Law

One of the most secret symbols in the lore of dynamic alchemy is the father devouring the son. When I first saw this, I immediately thought of mythology. A mythic god was warned by his parents that one of his children would dethrone him, so he devoured each child at birth. And who was this god? None other than Saturn, considered the oldest of the gods.

Later, while thinking about this symbol, I realized another significance: The Angel of the Presence, which the Saturn energy has been called, must "devour" the miscreating thoughts (children) of our fearful self-created "human" nature known as the Dweller on the Threshold; otherwise, the alchemical process will lose its power. And as you will see later, the part of Saturn that has received our projections of ignorance is indeed the Dweller.

Another alchemical symbol was two dead bodies having sexual intercourse in a coffin, which again is a secret referral to Saturn, who was said to spark creation from the death state—a seemingly lifeless or inactive state of consciousness. Saturn is a major link in the alchemical process because this energy represents the Law of Cause and Effect, the energy that "destroys what the lower nature has created and restores what the higher nature has envisioned so that the individual may have a more fulfilling life."[1] In the Ageless Wisdom texts, we find that "Christ (Jesus) . . . fulfilled the law under Saturn . . ."[2] And in *The Morning of the Magicians,* we read: "The old alchemical texts affirm that the keys to the secrets of matter are to be found in Saturn."[3]

When I wrote *The Angels Within Us,* I had no idea of the alchemical importance of Saturn at the time. He was shown only as the 22nd angel, the Angel of Success. I wrote:

> The astrological energy of Saturn used by this angel breaks up existing conditions by the force of its energy impact so that the higher ideals can be intuitively perceived. (It) is known as the Lord of Karma, the one who oversees the Law of Cause and Effect, ensures perfect balance, and forces us to prepare for the future.[4]

Now it is my understanding that after we took on physical bodies and began to lose our awareness of our Truth of Being—our reality as the Spirit-Sun of God individualized—the great Saturn archetype came forth to attach to and condition the personality, our self-image, how we and others see ourselves. In effect, Saturn became the Lord of each individual's physical-material world, and the function of Saturn—in oneness with the personality—was to be the Angel of the Presence, the law of perfect cause and perfect effect. By controlling the energy centers (chakras), Saturn rules the endocrine system and the entire organism, physiologically and psychologically, was maintained in a state of perfection. And for a time, there was nothing but Mind flowing into manifestation as heaven on earth.

But as we began to develop fear and self-preservation, this great archetype at one with the personal identity took on duality. It became both the Angel of the Presence and the Dweller on the Threshold—the sum total of both our God-created divine nature and our self-created ego.

Edwin Steinbrecher, the astrologer-metaphysician, found through research that this Saturnian energy has also been called "The Cosmos, the Crown of the Magi, the God of Fertility, Dominion or Slavery, and The Foundation of the Cosmic Elements and of the Material World."[5]

To the Hindus, this energy is Shiva, the destroyer of illusions; to the Hebrews, it was the Lord God, the power that restores the soul to its natural function of spiritual consciousness. "The Lord is my shepherd . . . he restoreth my soul." The early Gnostics called it the Workman, and Christian mystics considered the Saturnian energy as one of the seven spirits before the throne in Revelation.

In the symbology of the Tarot, this energy is the World, a card signifying the final and successful completion of any matter. It is fulfillment, the sum-total of creation. In *Highlights of the Tarot*, we read: "It shows that the dance of life is carried on by means of the form-building, solidifying power that gives us definiteness. . . . This power is the very basis upon which all science is founded."[6]

Isabel M. Hickey, the spiritual astrologer, wrote: "In understanding the mission of Saturn lies the solution to the mystery of life."[7] And "Saturn's goal is perfection."[8] Hickey also refers to Saturn as the "Lord of the World in us all. Keeper of the Records. Lord of Karma. Dweller on the threshold, but also the Angel of the Presence. Here is a mystery, and when one pierces through the veil, Saturn proves to be the Angel of Light that reveals the meaning of it all."[9]

Ageless Wisdom tells us that Saturn as the "Lord of the World" was also known as the *Ancient of Days*, a reference to Melchizedek, the king of Salem and priest of the Most High God. "You are a priest forever after the order of Melchizedek." (Psalm 110:4)

This is no ordinary energy that will serve as the positive force of the personality. According to the *Metaphysical Bible Dictionary*, *Salem* means "a consciousness of spiritual peace, wholeness, and perfection."[10] Saturn is the king of this consciousness. And to be a priest of the Most High God is to be an intermediary between Presence and Principle, a particular function of Saturn.

Remember that earlier you took on the energies of Power and Authority and Spiritual Strength and Will. This was the preparatory work for Saturn. The Aries energy reminded you of the key words, I AM, a greater sense of individual identity with more purpose and power in mind. And with the Leo energy of Spiritual Strength and Will, and its key words, I WILL, the heart is opened to greater courage and determination.

With these pronounced energy vibrations in consciousness, you are now ready to *consciously* become one with Saturn as the Angel of the Presence, to meet and commune with him (Saturn is an androgynous archetype but has appeared to me in masculine form), to *know* this angel and to work with mind and feeling nature until a firm relationship in consciousness has been established. The reason: This energy is the *Penetrating Law*, the impregnator of Creative Mind, and whatever is deposited in that receptive Sheath through the energy of Saturn forms the ideal pattern or matrix for manifestation.

So we want to take on the full power of this Light of the Lord, to literally become the Light so that we may experience the world that we have structured in our active imagination. We honor the Saturnian energy as ourselves and become the Law unto our world.

Let's pause for a moment here and eliminate any confusion or concern. I realize that it may sound strange to take on and become consciously one with what may be considered a mythological archetype, a particular planetary energy, or a symbolic entity from the mystical Tarot cards. But you should understand that this Living Energy called "Saturn" has been considered for eons as the perfecter of the personality and the true original nature of our conscious minds—the Angel of the Presence. In our conscious oneness with this power, fearfully negative thoughts flee; and we feel poised, whole, and complete. This is the attitude of mind we must have if we are to be successful in the alchemical process. Now, if the word *Saturn* bothers you and you find it difficult to divinely associate with what your conscious mind may identify as a "planet" or astrological energy, then call it by another name, such as the Angel of the Presence, the Angel of Light, or the Angel of Success and Fulfillment. However, for our purposes here, I will continue to use the Saturn designation.

Making Contact with Saturn

Ask your spiritual Guide to take you into deep inner consciousness, to personally escort you to meet with Saturn. As you draw close to the angel, notice as its light begins to take on form and features. The ancient symbolic picture of this archetype is a youthful figure with a feminine face and both a masculine and feminine body. Look into the eyes, and with great feeling in your heart, express your love and gratitude, and feel the love in return.

At this point, your intention is to merge consciously with this angel as you already are in reality. See yourself and the energy literally becoming one. It is the Angel of Light, the light shining into personal consciousness. Acknowledge the Source of the light, feel the radiation upon you as from a giant searchlight, the rays beaming in, around, and through you.

"Our individual mind is quickened to the extent that we make it receptive to the in-flooding of the light of Spirit."[11] You are this light, the light is you. Know and feel this. You now embody the Law of Cause and Effect *consciously*.

Say to yourself with great feeling:

I am the Angel of the Presence.
I am the Angel of Light.
I am the Angel of the Dawn.
I am the Energy of total and complete success.
I am the Law unto my world.

This step will also be repeated during the alchemical process, so practice the idea of *being* Saturn in consciousness, as the Light of God, as the loving Lord of your world. "The Lord consciousness is one of dominion. When we enter into our lordship, we rule. We rule over ourselves, our thoughts, our body, our environment, and all the creatures and creations of the earth."[12] This is the uplifted thought and feeling of poise, power, fearlessness, confidence, will, mastery, and dominion, all enveloped in an abiding consciousness of unconditional love. Do not forget the love. It is all-important.

✳✳✳

Chapter Six

Structuring Your Life with Saturn

tructuring begins with cleansing, and John Jocelyn's "A Saturn Song" seems appropriate here.

Man suffers most from what he fears;
He dreds the most what ne'er appears;
Thus does he often bear far more
Than God for him did hold in store.[1]

Functioning as the Law of Cause and Effect, our task now is to look at our "fears and dreds" and eliminate them once and for all. Simply put, we don't have to bear the burdens that we've assumed. They were self-created, not from God, and therefore were only phantoms of the mind claimed as real. Saturn knows this, and will help us know the truth that sets us free.

In our cleansing work, the first step is forgiveness without exception. We forgive ourselves and everyone within the range of our consciousness and beyond, including "this world." As I wrote in *The Superbeings:*

The word *forgive* means to "give up"—so you start cleaning up your mind by giving up all grudges and negative feelings toward others. All others. Everyone! Without exception. If you are holding any negative feelings about any individual or any group of people, stop right where you are, stir up that feeling of love within, and say, "I forgive you totally and completely."

As we probe deeper into our consciousness, we may see other negative thoughts hanging on for dear life. There's old Mr. Fear lurking in the background. You certainly don't want him around because you can't fear anything and also enjoy the experience of joyful living. So call in the Power of the Presence, and evict him now.

Ah, but there's a greenish hue of jealousy still remaining, plus a few mental delinquents called resentment, condemnation, prejudice, selfishness, guile, futility, deceit, inadequacy, impatience, irritation, and rejection. Getting rid of all of these delinquents one by one could be quite a chore, so let's just sweep them out all at once. "I call on the Law of Spirit now to arrest these intruders and take them out of my consciousness, out of my life, permanently. I don't need them. I don't want them. I will not have them!"[2]

Now meditate on these words with deep feeling:

Spirit of the living fire, pour Thyself on me that I may be consumed in the flames of purification. I cast all false beliefs into the all-consuming fire. I let all error thoughts burn in the purifying fire. I let my judging emotions pass away in the loving fire. I find my freedom in the cleansing fire. I see myself healed in the invisible fire. I rest in the living fire, and I become the spiritual fire.

We continue the cleansing of misqualified energy in the externals of life through denial. Catherine Ponder, a dear friend and famous inspirational author, writes about the prayer of cleansing in her book *The Dynamic Laws of Prayer:*

> All improved conditions in the world, with every step of progress from the beginning of time to the present, have resulted because someone said "no" to limiting appearances along the way and then worked to improve conditions.
>
> When you say to any apparent limitation of mind, body or affairs, "No, I do not accept this appearance. My life (health, wealth, happiness) cannot be limited!" you are dissolving fear. You are saying "no" to negative appearances. You are not accepting them, or giving them power, and so they have to fade away. The omnipresent good, which has been in your midst all the time, is then free to manifest as a happy result.[3]

Remember that Saturn is the great destroyer of limitations in your conscious mind, so in your oneness with that energy—feeling the power of total success which this energy represents—say "No!" to everything in your life that is below the divine standard of good, true, and beautiful. Pull the misqualified energy out from under the negative appearance, and watch it fade away. Keep in mind that the masterpiece of the perfect life cannot be created if you're looking in two directions at once.

Healing the Past

It is also important to heal the emotional memories of the past that still linger in consciousness because they can represent a major obstacle to health, wealth, and happiness. To do this, I recommend that you take a life-scan to rediscover events from the past that caused emotional scarring. Bring them up and remember in detail the situation; the people involved; the words spoken; the actions taken; and the consequences—in the form of fear, guilt, sorrow, embarrassment, and disappointment. Now rewrite the scenarios in your mind to see a different course of action resulting in love, harmony, and peace for all concerned. Keep editing the scenes until you are completely satisfied—*in your feeling nature*—with the outcome. Know that when you change your mind and feelings about an experience from the past, you are replacing the negative patterns on the unconscious level relating to that experience.

Continue the cleansing work daily, along with the following structuring activities to help you understand the divine aspirations that have been pressing on your heart.

✳✳✳

Robert Hand, author of *Planets in Transit*, says:

> Most people are out of touch with what they truly want. If you thoroughly understand your needs and wants, you will find that Saturn simply brings about their manifestation. . . . In a very real sense Saturn is the teacher, but it is each one of us teaching ourselves about what we really are.[4]

With Saturn *as* us, as the Light of Spirit *consciously*, let's teach ourselves what we really are with these ten structuring lessons:

1. Know your personality. As the old song puts it, "Accentuate the positive and eliminate the negative." What are your positive and negative points? Open your journal, and divide the page into two columns. On the left side write: "My

Positive Characteristics" and on the right: "My Negative Characteristics." Now search your mind and heart, and make your list with total honesty.

As you complete the list and look at both sides of the ledger, remember that Saturn can remove anything that hinders you from expressing the higher ideals. This Living Energy provides you with the opportunity for choices—to accept what is right and reject what is not, and upon rejection, the negative passes away; thus, it is "destroyed." Look again at your evaluation of yourself, and as the energy of Saturn, the Light of the Lord, choose and accept the positive characteristics as the structure of your personality, and reject the negative. Saturn will take it from there.

> *"Saturn is directly concerned with character building and is one of the greatest angels in the universe."* [5]

2. What do you value in life? In your journal, write what you consider "most important" in living a full and joyous life on Planet Earth at this time.

The key in this particular structure is to make the spiritual life the top priority without forgetting the importance of material forms and physical experiences. It is to be conscious of your Essential Self as the Reality of you, and seeing what you value in the objective world as a spiritual expression of that consciousness. It is the uniting of the inner with the outer, always knowing that the form as effect must follow Spirit as cause, yet not become less than Spirit in value.

> *"Saturn . . . demands acceptance of the material world as the temporary proving ground for the spirit."* [6]

3. Listen to your thoughts. This third structure is to become aware of your basic mind patterns. As Emerson wrote, "We are what we think about all day long." What are you thinking about most of the time? You may be surprised. I was when I began working with this exercise, and quickly had to bring in the denial of "No!"

Purchase a small pocket-size notebook or tape recorder, and carry it with you for a day. Every time you slip down into a lower frequency of mind and begin having thoughts of unworthiness, judgment, anger, jealousy, fear, guilt, or other less-than-divine attitudes, pause for a moment, say "No!" and then write or speak what you were feeling. At the end of the day, transcribe your findings to your journal, and ask the Saturn Light to dissolve this particular darkness in you.

"Saturn shows the weaknesses and lacks in the character so they can be changed into strengths." [7]

4. How would you evaluate your personal relationships? In this particular structure, the Saturn energy will show you the meaning and quality of true loving relationships. It will also reveal to you the people who should be brought into a closer bond of friendship with you, those to whom you should be more detached without violating the principle of unconditional love, and those relationships that should be ended for the good of all concerned while continuing to love unconditionally.

Become consciously aware of your oneness as Saturn, and then fill in the blanks below, or rewrite this information in your journal.

I reflect on the loving relationship I have with _____

Why do I consider this to be a loving relationship?

_____

_____

_____

_____

or

I choose a loving relationship with my true life partner,
and Saturn now shows me the vision of this ideal union.
(Write what you see.)

_____

_____

_____

_____

Saturn now shows me those who should be brought into
a closer bond of friendship with me:

_____

_____

_____

_____

Saturn now shows me those to whom I should be more de-
tached, without violating the principle of unconditional love:

_____

_____

_____

_____

Saturn now shows me those relationships that should be ended for the good of all concerned while continuing to love unconditionally:

_____

_____

_____

_____

"The 'losses' that Saturn brings are of things that you do not want or need. No matter how much you think you want them, let them go, especially relationships that Saturn may end." [8]

The above quote from Robert Hand in *Planets in Transit* should be looked at more closely. As surprising as it may seem, too binding a relationship with one's mother—particularly where there are strong reactive emotions—can be a barrier to living a prosperous life. According to esoteric astrologers and those who study the archetypes of the unconscious, the mother is the *mirror of prosperity* for her son or daughter. If you are continually seeking your mother's approval—your perception being that she does not regard with admiration what you are doing in life—you will carry that projection of her disapproval in your auric field. This will definitely affect your career, specifically in the area of finances.

If you think that in her mind you will never reach your full potential in life, that pattern of belief will screen out your abundance. If your family follows a fundamentalist religious faith where the mother is placed in a subservient position as the wife—not fully free to be herself—this view of limitation will limit your prosperity. The same thing applies if she believes that we are all here in physical form to suffer. Remember, she is the *mirror of your prosperity*. This is why the Saturn energy insists that you let go of all hindering relationships, even those considered most sacred—and the "ending" is nothing more than dissolving that part of the relationship mired in your emotional system.

Emotions relating to the mother always translate into materiality. To move past this, we should first understand that those feelings do not represent who we truly are and that we must cease identifying with them. They are nothing more than pockets of emotional energy that must be eliminated.

A friend told me that as a child he never felt he could please his mother—that he could do nothing right in her eyes. This caused an emotional block in him that severely restricted his ability to earn money as an adult. It was only after he brought up the repressed feelings and dealt with them that he found real prosperity. He said he rolled a piece of paper in the typewriter and wrote the story of his relationship with his mother from as early as he could remember. He focused on the emotional, verbal, and physical abuse; her hard, domineering presence; the feelings of ineptness and futility that she stirred in him; the turmoil in the home regarding her perceived lack of money; and the resentment she held toward his father for not providing enough. Every repressed emotion rose to the surface, and he let the anger engulf him in waves until it was finally dissipated. Then the tears flowed, and in time, there was a sense of peace. In essence, he ended what was a 40-year relationship filled with fear, guilt, and anger, and replaced it with divine indifference. He continued to love his mother unconditionally, but the emotional cord was cut, thus freeing both him and his mother.

I want to emphasize the importance of not looking at prosperity—or the lack of it—from your mother's perspective. She could be angry at those who "have more" or feel that money can only be earned by toil and being a slave to work—the old Puritan ethic—and as the mirror of your prosperity, you could play into that belief system. Also, do not get emotionally involved by looking upon your mother, especially if she is widowed, as living on a fixed income and not able to afford the finer things of life. This could result in a belief in limitation on your part, which will play out in some way to limit *your* income. See her as she is in truth—a treasure house of infinite riches, the lavish abundance of the universe in individual expression *as* her, with every need met easily and in peace. This impression on Creative Mind will work wonders for her, and will free you of any emotional involvement.

Oh, yes, how you feel about your mother-in-law is important, too, for she represents the *barometer of your career.* (The mother always represents prosperity; the mother-in-law mirrors your career.) So you should dissolve and heal that part of the relationship with her where there are emotional blocks. She is not doing anything to you; it is your emotional reaction to what you *think* she believes about you that is causing the problem. Cut the psychic cord and release the negative energy so that love, peace, and understanding become the bonds between you. Also consider how you are perceiving her. Is she successful in her activities of life? Again, see her as she is in truth, an instrument for the activity of Spirit, with full and joyous achievement.

5. Look at your creative activity. Saturn insists that you find something in life that truly delights you from the standpoint of originating, devising, designing, and making. It is bringing something into existence through your imagination and ingenuity that did not exist before. It could be a work of art, writings, unusual photographs, gardening, beautifying the home, creative cooking, or whatever else inspires you. The main thing is to select an activity and see it through with discipline, regardless of how difficult the project may be. This will open up new areas of creativity in mind, which will be important in the final creation of your Masterpiece for Life.

Make a list in your journal of things you would enjoy doing, select one, and make it your current project. Don't wait until you have more time. Do it now.

"Saturn focalizes on concentrated energy." [9]

6. Health of mind and body. This is a structuring of how you use your mind to positively affect the physical system, and how you are caring for the body with proper diet, exercise, vitamin supplements, and so on. You know that a spiritually positive attitude about this world, life in general, and you as a unique individual with a purpose for living directly influences the entire atomic structure of your body.

Ask yourself the questions shown below. If the answer to any of them is no, add a notation that from this day forward you will work with discipline to think, feel, speak, and act only from the highest frequency of consciousness.

* Am I honoring my body with right thinking on the One Life that is eternally whole?

* Have I transmuted reactive emotions of fear and anger into feelings of love and joy?

* Do I continually see the perfection I AM as God in radiant expression?

Then ask yourself: What can I do each day to live healthier with more energy and vitality? Write your responses in your journal.

"All disease is the result of inhibited soul life . . ." [10]

7. How is your social life? Do not dismiss this part of your life as something you don't need or as unimportant in your vision for a more fulfilling existence. We are social creatures, and if this aspect is afflicted, you are not going to enjoy the rich blessings that graciousness and cooperative interdependence can bring.

According to Plato, "True friendship is infinite and immortal." Do you have close friends who laugh and play with you, to break bread with in beautiful companionship, to listen to as they share their deepest feelings, and who respond to you with love and joy? That's life! That's living!

Jot down a few ideas of how you can improve your social life, remembering what Emerson wrote:

"The only way to have a friend is to be one."

8. Putting finances in divine order. Money is good. It is a spiritual idea in spiritual form, and therefore is unlimited. As you will see later, a vast fortune can be yours through the alchemical process, but for now, let's focus on your present financial situation.

Consciousness has a way of restricting money supply until there is greater order in financial management. It's that feast and famine thing. During the feast, times of plenty, we mismanage or get careless with our money, which causes a pocket of guilt to be deposited on the inner plane of consciousness. This naturally puts out a call for punishment (unconsciously), which then comes forth as a sentence of scarcity. We serve our time, make amends, and money is plentiful again, at least until the cycle repeats itself.

In this particular structure, we ask the question: What can I do to bring more order in my financial affairs? Write your answer in your journal.

*" . . . money is the consolidation of the loving,
living energy of divinity . . ."* [11]

9. What is your philosophy of life? What is life really all
about, and how is it to be lived—from your particular perspective? This calls for a very personal evaluation of your beliefs—of your hopes, wishes, and dreams. It is an opportunity
to lay the foundation for the kind (quality) of life you want to
live in this incarnation, which will become a major link in the
alchemical chain.

It is interesting that in earlier times, the words *philosopher*
and *alchemist* had the same meaning: *one who studied truth and
universal laws and applied the principles to life.* In essence,
philosophy is the system of beliefs through which we view life
in all its component parts to form a whole. With that as the start-
ing point, pause for a few moments in meditation on *My life
as* [your name]. See where your present reasoning has brought
you in terms of the basic attitude you hold toward life.

Now lift up your vision and see yourself living in what you
would consider the ideal state. What is the philosophical basis
for that view of life? Is it to live, love, laugh, and be happy . . .
to live and let live . . . to serve in the spirit of altruism . . . to
do everything for the joy of it. . . . to fulfill my divine purpose
. . .to make the best of that interval between birth and death?
Ponder the question, "What is my philosophy of life?" Form
the answer in your mind, and write it in your journal.

*"Well has it been said that no individual can suc-
ceed until he has developed his philosophy of life."* [12]

10. How do you wish to be known by the world? This
is not a tombstone inscription, but rather a narrowing down to

one specific answer that will be the foundation stone for your life's plan.

Write in your journal: *"I am the man, the woman, the person who* _____ *,"* and after a period of contemplation, fill in the blank.

"The only progress ever known was of the individual." [13]

The ten structuring lessons above will help you condition consciousness to be in greater alignment with the Saturn energy. Now before we go to the next link in the chain, practice again being one with this archetype. Remembering that you have taken on the conditioning energies of Power and Authority and Spiritual Strength and Will, say to yourself with feeling: *I AM . . . I WILL.* Now feel the light flowing in and from your Divine Self, and let yourself be bathed in that light. It is the Light of the Lord, the Angel of the Presence. Say:

I and the energy of Saturn are one.
I am the Light of the Lord.
I am the Angel of the Presence.
I am the Law unto my world.

✳✳✳

Chapter Seven

Veiled Isis: The Receptive Sheath

*T*he next major step in the alchemical process is to become aware of, understand, and intimately know the Veiled Isis, the Archetype of the hidden sanctuary of creative power. "Veiled" are the spiritual truths of the invisible worlds, and this shroud of obscurity is removed as we understand her function and secret processes.

In the Wisdom Teachings, we find that Isis was called the Virgin of the world. In her virginal state, she is penetrated by the Saturn-infused personality (the mind of will and choice). She then becomes pregnant with the manifesting ideas and takes on the role of the World Mother, the unveiled or known creative power, as we will discuss in the next chapter.

"Isis . . . is symbolic of receptive Nature—the watery, maternal principle which creates all things out of herself after impregnation has been achieved . . ."[1]

Also, "The mysteries of Hermeticism, the great spiritual truths hidden from the world by the ignorance of the world, and the keys of the secret doctrines of the ancient philosophers, are all symbolized by the Virgin Isis. . . . According to ancient philosophers, she personified Universal Nature, the mother of all productions. . . . The priests of Isis became adepts in the use of the unseen forces of Nature."[2]

In *The Woman's Encyclopedia of Myths and Secrets,* we read:

> The Hellenistic world identified "Isis of the Myriad Names" with every other female divinity. Medieval occultists in turn found her glorified in the writings of Plutarch and identified her with the World Soul, or Sophia. She appeared in numerous occult books as the Naked Goddess crowned with stars, her dominion over land and sea symbolized by her right foot on the earth, her left foot in water.[3]

Astrologically, this archetype is known as the Moon, representing the feminine or feeling nature. Isabel M. Hickey writes that "the Moon rules the form side of life and the functional activity of the body."[4] And the key words are *Matter, Maternalness, Receptivity, Feeling, Creativity,* and *Impressionability.*

Isis is symbolized in the Tarot as The High Priestess, the link between the spiritual and physical planes. Dr. Paul Foster Case, recognized world authority on the Tarot, says that "the High Priestess is a Virgin, and the blue color that predominates in this Key, as well as the flowing robe, represents Water. The curtain behind the High Priestess is a symbol of Virginity. It connects the two pillars of light and darkness, and all other pairs of opposites . . ."[5]

And according to Alfred Douglas, "The book or scroll she holds in her lap represents the mysteries of the hidden temple of which she is the guardian. . . . (She is) the channel whereby the divine is made manifest on earth."[6] Remember this point: *the channel whereby the divine is made manifest on earth.*

The Ancients said that the Moon is ruled by Saturn, and to use Edwin Steinbrecher's rather graphic terms, we see that Saturn is "the Woman with the Penis and the Old God," and the Moon is "the Vagina, the Goddess of the Night."[7] The dynamic alchemists said that in order to release the power into manifestation on the physical plane, there must be a "sexual affinity" with this aspect of creative law, which I interpret to mean a loving coupling, a passionate joining of energies.

In modern metaphysics, we find a so-called analogy with the conscious mind being the ruler or impresser of the subconscious mind, which receives the impression and immediately begins to create the pattern for manifestation. In a book on Hermetic Philosophy written in 1912 by Three Initiates, we find that "Thomas J. Hudson attained great popularity in 1893 by advancing his well-known theory of the "objective and subjective minds" which he held existed in every individual."[8]

This was another erroneous conclusion, one that diminished the *dynamics* of the alchemical process. If Hudson had been familiar with the original teachings of the alchemists—the theory of Mental Gender—he would not have formulated a new theory that reduced our basic divine constitution to nebulous psychological terms.

The authors go on to say that the duality of mind was a part of the ancient Hermetic teachings:

> The "I" represents the Masculine Principle of Mental Gender—the "Me" the Aspect of Becoming. The tendency of the Feminine Principle is always in the direction of receiving impressions, while the tendency of the Masculine Principle is always in the direction of giving out, or expression. The majority of persons really employ the Masculine Principle but little, and are content to live according to the thoughts and ideas instilled into the "Me" from the "I" of other minds.[9]

Let us also remember that rather than a "subconscious mind," which implies an aspect of a "human" mental nature, we have an aspect of God—the Feminine Principle of the Holy Spirit—functioning as our creative power. We are not all of God, but God is all of us!

In the Alice A. Bailey writings, Master Djwhal Khul says that the "Science of Impression is the mode of life of the subjective world which lies between the world of external happenings (the world of appearances and of exoteric manifestation) and the inner world of reality." [10] He also says that the "subconscious" is a terribly inadequate term, thus agreeing with the alchemists, yet he says that "the subjective realm is vitally more real than the objective, once it is entered and known. It is simply . . . a question of the acceptance, first of all, of its existence, the development of a mechanism of contact, the cultivation of the ability to use this mechanism at will, and then inspired interpretation." [11]

With Isis as this point of contact, rather than some indistinct submental phenomenon, we have a definite personality to interact with—an actual part of our spiritual constitution. This Moon Goddess is the essence, the essential character of our ME state—completely receptive to every heartfelt desire and ready to act on it. Working *as* Saturn, the Angel of Light, *with* Isis, the Receptive Sheath, you will create a paradigm so powerful that the manifestation of the ideal life cannot be delayed or denied.

It is time the courtship began.

Making Contact with Isis, the Moon Goddess

In your visit with Isis, she may very well take the form and appearance of her symbolic representation. The Ancients said she was the most beautiful woman in the world, and she may be seen sitting between two pillars wearing a blue flowing robe and a silver crown resting on her blonde hair. She has also been depicted as a lovely blonde maiden in a meadow, holding a flower in her right hand, a scroll in the other. And she has been seen in ancient times as a partially nude woman wearing a loose-fitting green garment. She could appear to you in other ways depending on the projections you're making upon her. To me, she appears as a radiant light filling the screen of my mind, and centered in this brilliance I see the facial features and the outlined shape of a female figure.

Your Spirit-Guide will escort you now to see this High Priestess. Relax, go into meditation, and ask that you may be taken to her. Feel the great love all around you as you make the inward journey. When you see the flickering light ahead, you will know that you are approaching this angel. As you come into her presence, look into her eyes and express your love with deep feelings. Tell her that you have taken on the Saturnian energy, the Angel of the Presence, as the identity of your personality, and that you will be working in a very close relationship with her to structure a new life for yourself. Ask for her cooperation in doing this. She will assure you that you have it, and may offer suggestions on how to visualize only that which is harmonious, beautiful, and noble in life. Write down what she says in your journal.

Isis works through three energy centers, initially through the solar plexus and heart, and later, after impression, through the throat chakra. Tell Isis that you want her to merge into your conscious awareness, to bring her light, her powers, her wisdom, and her very presence into a permanent state of reality in your mind and heart. Now see the bonding in the light; feel the vibrational change in your energy field as the light completely encircles your solar plexus and heart centers. Feel the warmth. Feel the love. Feel the passion.

Now speak words lovingly as you tell her how you will protect her and be her guardian.

From this day forward, I will do my very best to make sure that thoughts of discord and disharmony do not reach you.

With all my mind and heart, I will protect you from the negative forces of fear, anger, resentment, and guilt.

I will treat you with the respect of an aspect of my divinity, and will give you thoughts and feelings of only the highest order.

In turn, I ask that you be responsive to my will-for-good, which will be in harmony with universal truth, goodness, and beauty.

Now listen to her response, and write what you hear in your journal.

Making the "Marriage" Work

We know that "thoughts are things," or rather, they become the form and experience as they bear fruit. This takes us back to that earlier exercise—*what are you thinking about all day long?* Isis, the High Priestess of ME, takes these thoughts, particularly those that are trends of thought, and sets up a mental atmosphere, a pattern for the creative power. She does not reason or argue. Her mind method is deduction—that is, working from a premise to a logical conclusion. She takes what you give her and at once begins to build the inner design for the outer manifestation.

To work as a team for the highest good, you must change your attitude about life and stop complaining about what's happening "out there." Knowing that you have the power to change your world, you stop judging by appearances, see from the highest vision, and let Isis be impressed only with thoughts and feelings of Truth. And what is Truth? It means that wholeness, abundance, success, right relations, love, joy, and peace are part of the natural process of life, the natural laws of the universe. And that's what you concentrate on, knowing that this concentration infuses Isis, bringing forth the conception of the ideal.

Isis is completely in tune with these natural laws. Although she yields to your thoughts and feelings, she is one with Universal Mind that has no consciousness of scarcity, poverty, failure, futility, illness, or discord. She knows the lavishness of the universe, the extravagance of nature, the beauty of accomplishment and achievement, the truth of wholeness and perfection, and the harmony of loving relationships. That's her nature, and to impress any contrary ideas is to adulterate her energy.

The alchemists believed that the great percentage of our mental processes were continually taking place in the energy of the Moon within, and that if the individual was passive about this essentially unlimited power, life would "drift along" without purpose. They knew that this Archetype of ME looked to the authority of Saturn (I-mind in tune with the Saturnian energy) to direct her work with clear vision, courageous determination, and spiritual assertion. And the greater the work that we give her, the greater her performance.

She asks, "What do you will to be, do, and have?" She wants the Ideal as conceived in your mind—beautiful, opulent, complete—without any concern for present conditions. It doesn't make any difference if it's an *imagined* finished picture. To her it is real—not to come, but *now*. What do you see? What do you *want* to see? Hold it steady in mind, and let Isis build the mold for its manifestation.

Another point to bear in mind in the relationship is that she does not respond well to coercion, fearful pressures, or petulant persuasion. And if she takes on those vibrations from you, you will find your entire energy field in a downward spiral. Work with her with love, wisdom, spiritual vitality, great expectations, and feelings of joy and peace.

Feel her energy again encircling your heart and solar plexus, and gaze into her beautiful face. Lovingly converse with her, knowing that she will be ready and willing to accept the light of your Perfect World when you begin the alchemical process.

✻✻✻

Chapter Eight

Isis Unveiled:
The Creative Power

*A*n inscription carved above the figure of Isis at Nysa in Arabia reads: "I, Isis, am all that has been, that is or shall be; no mortal man hath ever me unveiled."

"Mortal man" with his fears and avarice could not probe the mysteries of this creative power and discover the keys to bring the invisible into visibility without suffering the backlash of chaos. Our intentions must be pure, our minds filled with a will-for-good, and our hearts on fire with love and feelings for the good of all. This is why it is said that *spiritual consciousness* must be the suitor, groom, and lover of this magnificent feminine energy. Then the veil is removed.

We have seen that the receptive Virgin, Isis, is impregnated by Saturn as the rule of law. What you, as the law, think into the energy of Isis results in an energy pattern through which she emanates as the creative power to fulfill the law. To understand this alchemically, think of it this way: In "the beginning," so to speak, the Love of God brought together two aspects of the Holy Spirit, producing a Force called the *World*

Mother. Joining in unity, in alchemical terms, were representative portions of the energy of Isis the High Priestess, and the energy of Venus the Empress—the latter also known as the Angel of Abundance and esoterically referred to as *Isis Unveiled.*

Keep in mind that as these energies became one, they also remained singular as the receptive sheath and the principle of supply to fulfill their particular functions. Yet together—the energies of Moon-High Priestess-Isis (veiled) combined with Venus-Empress-Isis (unveiled)—they formed the great Mother Goddess. "She embodies the super-abundant creative forces of nature, together with the benign feminine wisdom of the Queen of Life. Her concerns are essentially those of the physical plane." [1] Isis unveiled is the Mother who gives birth to the idealized form or experience through emanation.

Emanate comes from the Latin word meaning "to flow." The Egyptian alchemists believed that the connecting link between spirit and matter was the emanation (the flow) of the Great Thought, female. Bring to mind again the feeling-knowing of being the Holy Sun of God. See the sun in the sky representing an image of how your individual energy field appears. From this magnificently brilliant Force Field you are, the World Mother—who materializes all things that have a beginning and an end—shines forth as light, love, substance, supply, and the very grace of God.

Isis unveiled as the World Mother is also known alchemically as the third divine "person," referred to here as the Activity of God. Do not confuse this with the "Voice for God" in other spiritual literature. That mediator between illusion and truth is another aspect of the Holy Spirit, the Energy of Creative Intelligence that does not become involved with the material world.

The musical note of Isis unveiled as World Mother is *Fa*, the key of F. (Do Re Me *Fa* is C D E *F*) We come into greater alignment with her emanation when we hum that note. Find it on the piano or pitch pipe, and practice the sound. (All of the sound and imaging exercises mentioned here are an important part of the preparation stage for alchemy, but they will not be used in the actual process.)

The Mother's symbol is the square, indicating the fourth aspect of Spirit as Spirit becomes matter, the manifest form. It is also interesting that in esoteric astrology, the square relates to *material appearance*, the expression of form. Hum the sound of *Fa* while visualizing a square, and write in your journal what appears in the square.

Keep in mind that the feminine creative power of the Mother absorbs the mental atmosphere charged with feeling, the pattern for expression, and the design for manifestation. She then radiates into the phenomenal world specifically through the throat chakra, the organ for the distribution of creative energies.

Bring in the sound of *Fa* and the image of the square while you are feeling the flow of creative power through your throat as a simultaneous activity. Describe the sensation and images in your journal.

Vitvan, the great American Master and founder of the School of the Natural Order, says that we should think of the World Mother according to three different aspects:

> The first aspect we describe as magnetic-energy or substance in a state of activity but *undifferentiated,* or as undifferentiated Light.
>
> The second aspect we describe as magnetic-energy *differentiated* as patterns, designs . . .as lines of force within a field forming a pattern, making a design.

The third aspect respecting the magnetic-energy or World Mother-substance we describe as configurations or energy-forms. Upon weblike patterns determined by the lines of force describing the energy-fields, or like pearls upon a string, units of energy configurated.[2]

Vitvan also writes:

This world is an energy-world, a vast energy-system; all that we have heretofore called things and objects are in reality configurations or units of energy effected or brought about by the formative forces of the World Mother.[3]

Focus on the power radiating from your throat center and say to yourself with feeling:

The formative force of abundance is flowing through me now.
The formative force of success is flowing through me now.
The formative force of wholeness in body is flowing through me now.
The formative force of right relations is flowing through me now.

At every moment in time and space, the World Mother is flowing, pouring, radiating, and shining forth from the deep impression you have made upon her virginal state; and goes before you to create anew for you, or attract that which is already manifest for your use. Her power is omnipotent, her supply unlimited, her energy infinite. You cannot stop the flow or obstruct it in any way. She flows unceasingly—and impersonally—to express as gladness or madness, abundance or poverty, health or sickness, success or failure, harmony or conflict. She fulfills the law initiated by your thoughts and feelings and impregnated within her receptive sheath.

Vitvan says that "each individual represents the Great Mother, as a focalization of magnetic solar-sphere energies . . . he functions with the forces and energies of the World Mother."[4] He suggests that we orient ourselves as a focalization of these energies and become consciously aware of the constant activity of the Mother in and through us. We do this through loving gratitude, and by seeing her activity not only as creative manifestation, but also as the power that goes before us to straighten out the crooked places, perfect that which concerns us, and perform that which is ours to do.

The Tibetan Master, Djwhal Khul, has written:

> It is here that many mystics prove futile. They work from far too high a level and from the standpoint of spiritual incentive. They normally and naturally (because that is where their focus of consciousness is placed) work from the standpoint of the second aspect, the Christ Self, whereas it is the third aspect (equally divine and equally important) which must be invoked and evoked. . . . It is . . . the relating of physical need and physical supply and the bringing together of two tangibles through the power of creative imagination. It is for this reason that so many schools of thought prove so successful in materializing that which is required, and why other schools of thought so significantly fail.[5]

The Christ Self is the domain of Truth, of Divine Ideas, and of infinite Knowingness. It is the Spirit of God within in the Absolute and does not become involved with the effects of the phenomenal world. Our work with Spirit is to know this Divine Identity as ourselves—to unify with the Great I AM as the Truth of Being, and to receive and accept Its shining Light of Divine Mastery.

As I pointed out earlier, we begin on that high plane as the Divine Self and take that awareness with us as we move through the links in the alchemical chain, ultimately focusing on the emanation of the third aspect, knowing that the Mother is the agent of manifestation on the material plane.

As the energy of Saturn, the Light of Spirit, we give the creative mind of ME the right materials to build the framework for life's masterpiece, and then we focus our mind on the flowing all-inclusive supply that brings it all to pass in ideal form and experience. And in that energy stream of the Mother, we see the unity of spirit and matter. We see-feel the lavish abundance of money as spirit in form. We see-feel the great success in life as spirit in experience. We see-feel everything good in life as the Mother gives birth to every hope, wish, and dream.

Before we move to the next chapter, take time to sit quietly for a few minutes in imaginative meditation. Acknowledge your Holy Self as you move from above your head down to the encircled heart and solar plexus centers. Now move up and feel the creative power radiating out through your throat chakra. See it going before you in a continuous stream of golden energy, and in that river of gold, see the energy configurations coming together as form. Connect mind and matter, spirit and form. See lavish amounts of money in the energy stream, the symbols of your success, the perfect love-mate, home, transportation, and anything else you desire. See energy creating (or attracting) out of energy—the form, experience, condition, or situation. See your ideal life in a world of energy where every possibility in heaven and earth exists.

With this exercise, you are practicing seeing the flowing energy and the form or experience simultaneously. W. Frederic Keeler put it this way, using money as an example:

> What brings the Abundance that is of Spirit and of Truth
> into tangible money? Here is the point of bringing about its

manifestation. One must believe as much in money as one believes in Spirit, God. That belief raised to Faith and Knowing constitutes metaphysical power regarding it.

Belief in Spirit does not of itself produce money. Belief in visible things does not produce, although it may accumulate things. Belief in both . . . each for the other, each transformable and transferable into the other, each harmoniously related to the other . . . such belief brought to perfection as a unity in thought and intelligence, brings the desired manifestation.[6]

As you will soon see, this "unity of thought" is of vital importance in the alchemical process.

✳✳✳

Chapter Nine

Achieving Right Understanding

*E*arlier I said that we give the Creative Mind, Isis, the right materials to build the framework for life's masterpiece. And the right materials include right understanding, which leads to right thoughts, which begets right words and actions. Remember, we are what we think about all day long, or as the Buddha stated it:

> *"All that we are is the result of what we have thought. If a man speaks or acts with an evil thought, pain follows him. If a man speaks or acts with a pure heart, happiness follows him, like a shadow that never leaves him."*

To help us in our understanding of God, Life, and Law, let's look at a few more of the Hermetic Principles from the original alchemists.

1. "The All is Mind; the Universe is Mental." — the *Kybalion*

And it has been written by an old Hermetic Master ages ago that "he who grasps the truth of the Mental Nature of the Universe is well advanced on The Path to Mastery."[1]

There is but one Mind, one Power, all Divine. We use the same mind and power in our individual worlds that the All did in creating the universes. By thought and word, the Masculine Presence (God) activated the Feminine Principle (Goddess) and brought forth all living things. And we, in oneness with this Union of Presence and Principle, follow the same creative process in manifesting our Perfect World.

Presence plus Principle equals Life, and Life is omnipresent, which means that all things *live*. Life created a universe of Life, and out of this Life, we, as individuals stepped forward as Life in radiant expression. That expression is self-knowing, the ability to think and to create in the microcosm (this world) as the All does in the Macrocosm (universal).

2. "While All is THE ALL, it is equally true that THE ALL is in ALL. To him who truly understands this truth hath come great knowledge." — the *Kybalion*

Think of the individualizing process again, as the universal Masculine-Feminine Spirit expresses or becomes the Shining Sun of God, the I AM embodying the fullness of the Godhead. We are the Allness of God in individual expression, a unity of Presence, Mind, and Principle—the All Power, the only Power.

Say to yourself:

> *I AM the Spirit of the Living God.*
> *I AM the Self-Knowing Mind of Spirit.*
> *I AM the Creative Power of Spirit.*

Spirit, Mind, and Power as a Cosmic Unit completely surrounds, fills, and encompasses what we know as our individual energy field. The Allness of God is fully present where we are, and as Who and What we are.

3. "Every Cause has its Effect; every Effect has its Cause; everything happens according to Law; Chance is but a name for Law not recognized; there are many planes of causation, but nothing escapes the Law." — the *Kybalion*

The universes were created by and through Law, Law being the *how* of the creative process. It is the unvarying uniformity of divine order based on the principle of cause and fundamental truth. That which is visible is an effect of cause, creative mind, which is Law.

Our minds are creative and follow the same cause-and-effect process. We live in a world of law and order, and it is impossible that any force can be exerted without a corresponding effect. Therefore, we are constantly creating, by law, our individual worlds. We are the masters of our fate, the captains of our soul.

How are you using the law? What are you consistently thinking about? You are what you think into the receptive sheath of Feminine Mind. Remember that the Saturnian energy is the energy of success, and success is the tone, pitch, shape, and quality that should be pulsating in your consciousness. And what is success? Ageless Wisdom tells us that success is the *natural order*, that we are here in physical form to attain mastery over the manifest world, to triumph over everything considered the opposite of success: failure, lack, limitation, downfall, conflict, hostility, and infirmity. Total success is the kind of thinking that the I must impress upon the ME.

4. "Nothing rests; everything moves; everything vibrates." — the *Kybalion*

Looking at this axiom from the standpoint of individual being, we see that in each particular energy field there is a vibration of either attraction or repulsion based on the thoughts that have built up over time. These thoughts are both conscious and unconscious, and on each level, creative action is taking place. With the Saturn influence, you are beginning to control your conscious thoughts by focusing only on what you want to experience, thus moving into a more spiritual vibration.

When negative emotions arise from the unconscious plane that tell you otherwise, you are counterbalancing with a denial (No!). You resume the position of self-mastery by moving up quickly to a deep and abiding awareness of your Divine Consciousness, which changes your vibration, and the offending emotion passes from you. This steady focus (contemplative meditation) on the Truth of Being will erase all below-the-surface error patterns from the past.

You have the power of will and choice, so will and choose to think, feel, and see only that which is ideal in life. This moves you into the Master Vibration. Don't dwell on the past, and don't even think about the possibility of scarcity, failure, or misfortune in the future. All the power of the universe is with you, in you, and is forever seeking, by law and will, its own level—its Divine Standard of abundance, success, and fulfillment in your life.

Keep the truth fixed permanently in your mind that the Light of the Lord influence (Saturn) gives you Divine Ambition, the discipline to achieve it, and the opportunities for grand accomplishment.

5. Everything is dual; everything has poles; everything has its pair of opposites; like and unlike are the same;

opposites are identical in nature, but different in degree; extremes meet; all truths are but half-truths; all paradoxes may be reconciled." — the *Kybalion*

This is the Principle of Polarity, which the Ancients said was the secret of manifestation. And what is polarity? Webster defines it as "opposite magnetic poles; and any tendency to turn, grow, think, feel in a certain direction." The alchemists knew that the law of manifestation depends upon polarity, that a circuit (a path over which energy may flow) must be formed. But the circuit cannot be formed unless we operate in harmony with the law.

"If your thought is in harmony with the creative Principle of Nature, it is in tune with Infinite Mind, and it will form the circuit . . . but it is possible for you to think thoughts that are not in tune with the Infinite, and there is no polarity; the circuit is not formed."[2]

The alchemists said that poverty and abundance, failure and success, illness and health, and any other pair of opposites are all poles of the same thing, with many degrees between them. Accordingly, by raising your mental vibrations, you will polarize along the lines of the fulfillment you seek. How do you raise your vibrations? By thinking and seeing your individual world from the vantage point of your Divine Consciousness. It may be necessary to use your imagination at first, but Spirit will quickly take over and show you the Truth, the Reality, of your life from the higher knowing. And in that vision, there is only vibrant well-being, loving relationships, an all-sufficiency of money, creative achievement, and a life so beautiful, so filled with wonder. See as Spirit sees, and feel the dynamics as you are lifted to a higher polarity.

When this polarization happens, the circuit is formed between the Masculine and Feminine Principles of your being, the I and the ME. The currents of thought then flow easily from the arena of will and choice to the receptive vessel of creative power—and your life immediately begins to reflect this inner glory.

6. "The truly wise . . . by the Art of Alchemy transmute that which is undesirable into that which is worthy, and thus triumph." — the *Kybalion*

You cannot triumph over conditions by thinking and feeling what is undesirable. If you think illness, you cannot demonstrate health. If you feel scarcity, abundance is repelled. That is the law. Change the way you think and feel, always focusing on what you wish to experience, and the Great Creative Mother, as Law, will show you that nothing is impossible.

Also, remember that if you do not expand your thinking (infinite possibilities) and increase your positive feelings (love, joy, gratitude), you will become stagnant, stale, and enter into a state of inertia. There is always a step beyond just doing fine, feeling better, or being satisfied. The Feminine Principle has no limits on creativity, manifestation, and attraction.

With our pursuit of understanding, let's turn our attention again to the veiled and unveiled Isis, the great Creative Mother-Mind.

First, in what we think of as "the beginning," Positive Father-Will activated the Magnetic Mother-Power, and a universe was born. "The Bible's highly derivative version says 'the earth was without form, and void; and darkness was upon the face of the Deep' (Genesis 1:2). The Deep was the Mother's womb, *tehom*, derived from Tiamat, the Babylonian name of the primordial Goddess."[3]

And the Earth within the infinite sphere blossomed with vegetation and living creatures. Creation continued as the thought and word of I-Will penetrated the ME-Power to produce an archetypal pattern of individualization, a union of the

Cosmic Mother and Father. As Vitvan states it, ". . . fixing attention upon the cosmic process . . . we see that it is the World-Mother in the virgin state (undifferentiated) which by union with the Positive Power conceives and gives birth to the Son (individual)."[4]

It is this Feminine Principle in and shining forth from each individual that is not only the causative source of all manifestation, but is also the kingdom or inexhaustible treasure house of all that you could possibly want, need, or desire. As the ME of you, she expects you to work with her in continuing the creative process of bringing heaven to earth—the manifestation of your Perfect World as seen in the High Vision and etched in your mind of will and choice. In her infinite intelligence, she knows the answer to every question, the solution to every problem, and the how and way of every accomplishment. She gave birth to the universe and this world, and through the same omnipotence will bring your Ideals into perfect form and experience.

This Mother-Spirit not only fashioned your physical body, but also functions as the continuing healing presence, maintaining the physical system in harmonious wholeness—unless you counteract her natural tendencies through negative thought patterns. By cancelling out false impressions through will, decision, and choice, her expressions—as the Life Principle—will once again positively affect every atom, cell, tissue, and organ of your body and restore you to perfect health.

Remind yourself often that this healing power, this manifesting agent, is not something separate and apart from you. It is the feminine aspect of your very being, the Goddess of Creativity and Attraction, the ME of you. And she seeks your trust, faith, and confidence in her and asks only that your thoughts and feelings be constructive rather than destructive. As Law, she will move in either direction; but as Love, her natural inclination is toward that which is good, true, and beautiful in life.

Feelings of good health, regardless of appearances, produce a state of wholeness. To her, radiant well-being is your natural state, unless you think otherwise. Feelings of wealth trigger an outpouring of visible money supply. She doesn't believe in just enough to go around, unless that is your decision. Feelings of success bring forth experiences or achievement and accomplishment, of true place in life. She thrives on victory and triumph, but will honor your claim of futility and failure.

And what are you *seeing*? Active imagination or controlled visualization galvanizes the Mother-Spirit into action to bring this blueprint in mind into reality. She takes the raw material that you give her in feelings and mental images and builds the perfect pattern, then literally pours her energy through the pattern into the ideal manifestation on the physical-material plane.

Another crucial point: When you think of another person in any particular way, the Feminine Principle in you picks up the vibration as though you are thinking about yourself, for to her, the selfhood is united as one. If you see someone as ill, poor, a victim of circumstance, or in other downward visioning, you are calling for that experience personally. The Wise Ones in 500 B.C. knew this and gave us the Golden Rule, which was later incorporated into the Bible. What you do to others in thought, feeling, and word, you are doing to yourself. To express goodwill toward others and honor their Truth of Being—whole, rich, and triumphant—you are invoking the Creative Mother to multiply the good in your life. This is the key for loving and harmonizing relationships with everyone, to see in them what you want for yourself—joy, love, peace, and fulfillment.

The same principle holds true when you are overly critical of yourself. A silent, invisible vibration goes out to others that actually repels, for to judge yourself as less than divine is to pass judgment on everyone else—and they will pick it up in their feeling nature. Admit to any mistakes you may have made, forgive the ego thoughts that created them, and let all self-grievances be replaced with love. Find that Point of Innocence within you, and ME will show it to the world.

When we begin the alchemical process and work with imaging, feelings, and words, it is important to remember to stay relaxed. Pressure, strain, or mental effort will be counterproductive. The greater the ease, the greater the reception by Isis. In fact, she comes closer to the surface of consciousness when you are in a state best described as "meditative serenity." Again, you are not using willpower; you are expressing your will through choice, effortlessly.

✻✻✻

Chapter Ten

Thoughts of Truth, Words of Power

*I*f we are going to maximize our potential as dynamic alchemists, we must condition the mind of will and choice with ideas and concepts that are in tune with eternal truths. Then we will *believe* what we are thinking, *believe* the words we are speaking, *believe* what we are impressing upon the World Mother. We can think or say, "I can't be sick," "I am rich," and "Success is mine," but if we do not consciously *believe* what we are affirming, the whole process is short-circuited because the Feminine Principle only acts on what we believe is true.

Health and Wholeness

It has been taught for eons that the Mother-Spirit, the Feminine Principle of our soul, created our physical bodies. In her infinite intelligence, she fashioned the entire atomic structure, forming cells, tissue, organs, bloodstream, bones, and the various life-giving systems. There is nothing that she does not know about the body, which means that she is also the healing principle when something in the system gets out of balance through negative thought patterns. In other words, she knows what to do! Accept this as an absolute truth, and believe in her power.

Speak these words of power with quiet assurance, and feel the truth in your heart center as a deep pulsation of love and gratitude:

> *The Creative Mother is now healing my mind of all false beliefs and error patterns, and is restoring and maintaining my body in perfect health.*

Now lift up your vision and see yourself as you want to be in your active imagination, remembering that this is the image you are conveying to your feeling nature, rather than what appears to be a problem.

> *I see myself with a magnificently healthy body in perfect order, where every cell is in the image of the perfect pattern, and I am whole and complete. I see myself as vibrant, energetic, and filled with a new zest for life. I feel wonderful!*

If there is by chance even the slightest blip of denial of the words and image, then raise your vibration and think from the level of your Holy Self. English psychologist Charles F. Haanel writes:

> The affirmation, "I am whole, perfect, strong, powerful, loving, harmonious and happy" will bring about harmonious conditions. The reason for this is because the affirmation is in strict accordance with Truth, and when truth appears, every form of error or discord must necessarily

disappear. You have found that the "I" is spiritual; it must necessarily then always be no less than perfect. The affirmation is therefore an exact statement.[1]

To believe what we are thinking, imaging, and saying is so vitally important. *Do not fear, only believe.* (Mark 5:36) *All things are possible to him who believes.* (Mark 9:23) *Therefore I tell you, whatever you ask in prayer, believe that you have received it, and it will be yours.* (Mark 11:24)

Believe, believe, believe! And this is where the infusion of the Saturn energy can be so beneficial. This Lord of the Light works with our conscious mind to help us see and understand the truth—the truth that health is the natural state, that wealth is a natural right, that success is a universal principle, and that loving relationships are divinely ordained as law. We are here to reveal a Perfect World based on the eternal verities of life, and this Angel of the Presence will show us that indeed, all things are possible.

Take on the energy of that Angel now and say, believing:

> *I am the law of health unto my physical system,*
> *the cause of the mental currents being received by*
> *the Creative Mother. I send forth only thoughts,*
> *words, and images that are harmonious, peaceful,*
> *loving, and true.*

Understanding the principle that things equal to the same thing are equal to each other, state the following axioms, which will be accepted by Creative Mind and brought forth into manifestation.

> *Spirit and Life are synonymous.*
> *I am Spirit;*
> *Therefore, I am Life.*

Life, being of God, is perfect.
The Life within me is perfect;
Therefore, my body partakes only of perfect Life.

I am a spiritual being with a physical form.
That form is fashioned after the perfect Life pattern;
Therefore, my body is perfect and is in a state of
complete healthfulness.

There can be no argument here, because regardless of appearances, you are thinking-speaking the truth. You have established a solid basis for reasoning that you can consciously believe, and this belief is readily accepted by Creative Mind.

The Principle of Abundance

The universe of infinite plenty assures us that enjoying wealth on the material plane is not only our right and duty, but is the law. In other words, we *must* be rich—not as a possibility, but as a *certainty*. It is the same as any other rule or governing principle: *That's the way it is.* Of course, it is possible to overcome or break the law. For example, an airplane overcomes gravity to leave the ground; we break the law of abundance through ignorance or fear of scarcity.

The Creative Mother, the ME of you, never considers economic situations. All she knows is boundless, unlimited abundance, and by law seeks to manifest infinite riches in the material world. She is a literal gold mine, forever producing lavish, overflowing wealth in all its many forms.

In Roman times, money was considered a gift from the Goddess, and was considered holy. Even the writers of the Bible recognized that being prosperous was equivalent to a life of beauty, happiness, and freedom.

Beloved, I wish above all things that thou mayest prosper. (3 John 2)

Whatsoever he doeth shall prosper. (Psalms 1:3)

Peace be within thy walls, and prosperity within thy palaces. (Psalms 122:7)

The pleasure of the Lord shall prosper in his hand. (Isaiah 53:10)

So shall my word . . . prosper in the thing whereto I sent it. (Isaiah 55:11)

The God of heaven, he will prosper us. (Nehemiah 2:20)

Thou shalt remember the Lord thy God, for it is he that giveth thee power to get wealth. (Deuteronomy 8:18)

It was only after the early Christians heard that the pagans equated money with sex (the old masters knew it was based on the same energy) did Paul write "money is the root of all evil." (1 Timothy, 6:10) The ancient mythological belief was that the essence of silver and gold was the spirit of eroticism, and this obviously bothered Paul and influenced his views on both sexuality and money.

Now, what can you consciously believe is true regarding abundance in your life? You can look through spiritual eyes and see the truth that scarcity cannot exist in your life because it does not exist anywhere in the universe. And neither does the appearance of loss. There is no lack or limitation anywhere. Understand this.

You can also merge in conscious awareness with the Mother-Spirit and realize that *you* are the infinite Treasure House of Riches, which will help you to polarize in the higher vibration. And consider what words of power you can use to convey the right impression on the creative medium, such as:

There is always an abundance of money.

This is absolutely true considering the monetary resources of the world, of which you are a part. You are not saying that you, personally, always have a surplus of money, which you do not believe. You are stating simply, *There is always an abundance of money*—a fact that is easily received by the feeling nature.

Now think about Mother Nature and her manifest extravagance, and say:

I live and move and have my being in lavish abundance.

That's another truth that can be accepted. Also remember that the Creative Mother, your Feminine Principle, is the individualization of Universal Mother Nature, whose vast scheme of creation and reproduction is continually at work. Get this firmly in mind, then say:

I cannot be limited, for I am the law of expansion, increase, and fruition. A magnificent harvest of excess is springing forth at every moment, ready for gathering. I am the Spirit of Infinite Plenty. I am the Shining Sun of Supply, and God's wealth fills my world.

Isis knows that with such words of power, you are referring to yourself as her, as the World Mother, and she will respond accordingly.

Success

We will work a bit differently in the area of success. Success is based on the ideal *to do, to be*—that which you passionately want to achieve and accomplish. What is your image of true success? That which you can conceive in mind as the ideal goal in life, your master intention, must already be a part of your consciousness; otherwise, you could not conceive of it as a possible reality.

Think now, what is the Divine Purpose of your life? Ask to be shown through the higher vision. What do you see? Open your intuitive faculty and feel Spirit's pressing to reveal what you can do to provide maximum service to this world. Determine what you want to be and do for the good of all, and fill in the blanks below.

*My ideal is to be a*_____

*My purpose in life is to be a*_____

*My intention is to be the best*_____
I can be.

Get your fixed purpose in mind, hold it there, and see it in total completeness. Feel the thrill of victory, the vitality of triumph, and let the Feminine Principle be impressed with the high vision and the joy of fulfillment. There is not a "roll of the dice" here. You are consciously controlling your destiny, for what you see, you shall become. The vision will be made real.

Contemplate these truths, adapted from the Angel of Success meditation.[2]

*All that the Universal Presence of God has is
mine, for God and the expressions of God cannot be*

*separated. They are forever one, and therefore I live
in the Eternal Now with the Infinite All, and nothing
is missing in my life. I AM the power of God to
HAVE.*

*I am the fiery strength of God, the living force of
vitality that goes forth with divine intention and authority. My creativity is Love in action, and everything I do is victorious. My divine power is the
thought that I WILL, and every door swings open
before that power.*

*I have divine aspirations to fulfill my highest
destiny, and with enthusiasm I move forward, forever
illuminated by the higher vision. I see that which is
mine to do, and I do it with ease, devotion, and gladness, and I am blessed with the treasures of heaven,
for that is what I SEE.*

*I walk in the footsteps of my Self, and my path is
sure. My ideals have been formulated in the crucible
of my mind and are forged in divine design in my
heart. In joyful freedom, I now follow my heart, for
I have seen my destiny, and what I see, I KNOW.*

*I am enjoying the fullness of unlimited success,
for I am in my true place, doing what I love and loving what I do, for the good of all. I am the spirit of
accomplishment, the force of achievement, and every
activity of my life now reflects the ideals of victory,
beauty, harmony, and abundance, for that is what I
BELIEVE.*

As you move through the day and on to the busy thor-
oughfares of life, keep the ideas in mind about success that you
can consciously believe, thus eliminating any barriers to the
right impression on the Mother-Spirit. Formulate your own be-
lief-affirmations, with these as starters:

I am the consciousness to do, be, and have.
I am the power to be successful.
I am the energy of success.
The creative activity of God is flowing through
me now, and my mind is responsive to divine
thoughts of success.
I have made a firm and definite decision in my
mind to be wonderfully successful. I now accept the
truth that the spiritual idea of True Place Success,
the Divine Plan for me, is right where I am.

You might also think about what some great minds have
written about success:

"Have a purpose in life, and having it, throw
into your work such strength of mind and muscle as
God has given you." — Carlyle

"The surest way not to fail is to determine to
succeed." — Sheridan

"Nothing succeeds so well as success."
— Talleyrand

"I believe the true road to preeminent success in
any line is to make yourself master of that line."
— Andrew Carnegie

"We can do anything we want to do if we stick to
it long enough." — Helen Keller

"If a man can write a better book, preach a
better sermon, or make a better mousetrap than his
neighbor, though he build his house in the woods,

the world will make a beaten path to his door."
— Emerson

It is also important to etch deeply in the great creative medium of ME the truth of your worthiness to achieve and accept magnificent success in life. Work with this meditative treatment:

> *I recognize my value as an individual being living on earth at this time. As the very worthiness of God, I am part of the Grand Plan of continuing creation, and my contribution to this world is vitally important in the divine scheme of things.*
> *Poised, powerful, and peaceful, I do my part with love and joy. I am guiltless, open, and receptive to right action, and devoted to my purpose in life. Everything I do is meaningful and worthwhile. I am deserving because I know who I am.*

Relationships

What can you believe about relationships? What truths can you impress upon Isis in terms of your association with other people? It all begins with the word *love*. In *Living a Life of Joy*, I wrote:

> We live and move and have our being in the energy of love. We breathe love, our bodies are sustained by love, and our Life Force is pure love. We can't get out of love—it's omnipresent. We can't out-think love—it's omniscient, and as it's omnipotent, we can't overpower it. It is the single force of universal Cause, and its permanent home is within each one of us. We are eternally the fire and flame of divine love

burning brightly, the light of God-love shining throughout every dimension. I AM perfect love is the truth of the ages.[3]

Ageless Wisdom tells us that love is harmony, that harmony is a universal principle, and that a harmonious relationship with everyone is a part of the natural process of life. Therefore, the Creative Feminine of ME works on this tone or chord as law, and to give her thoughts and feelings of discord and conflict in your attachment to others will produce intense agitation and reverse her normal action of maintaining amicability, friendship, and cooperation.

As the Bible states it, *"So whatever you wish that men would do to you, do so to them, for this is the law . . ."* (Matthew 7:12) And *"Judge not, that you be not judged. For the judgment you pronounce, you will be judged, and the measure you give will be the measure you get."* (Matthew 7:1-2) What you give out in thoughts and feelings toward another, you get back—usually multiplied.

Now back to those thoughts of truth and words of power:

Love is the greatest power in the universe, freely given to one and all.

God loves me, and through God's love, I can love others.

As I judge others, I am judged.

As I love others, I am loved.

My harmonious thoughts are returned in kind.

What I am feeling about another, I am feeling about myself. I choose to only feel peacefully and lovingly toward all.

What I want for myself, I want for everyone.

I practice harmlessness in thought and feeling each and every day.

Begin this day to make friends with everyone in your family, seeing the truth in them and loving and honoring their divinity. Then see and feel only harmony with those in the workplace, and expand the circle to encompass everyone on this planet and beyond. Your ideal life has no room for friction, unpleasant thoughts about others, resentment, or hostility. Your intention should be to be at peace with everyone, and for everyone to be at peace with you. And this is not idealistic. The Mother-Spirit, functioning from the point where you are and reaching out into omnipresence, will gladly fulfill the natural law of love, harmony, and peace if you will give her that impression from your mind and heart.

Contemplate these thoughts to condition your consciousness:

If there has been any disharmony in my life, it shows me that I haven't loved enough, for love is the correcting principle of the universe. When I truly love and let it flow, it goes before me to straighten every crooked place. I let it be done.

My inner Light now draws to me those with whom I can relate in love, peace, and joy. Because it is the principle of right relations in action, my desires are beautifully fulfilled, my needs easily met.

Creative Mind is forever securing the bond of harmlessness and harmony between me and everyone else in my world. Therefore, I am totally confident to let God appear as each and every relationship in my life.

The activity of divine attraction and right relations is eternally operating in my life.

If a soulmate or life partner is part of your perfect world— and you desire this intimate relationship—then realize the truth that somewhere, right at this moment, there is the ideal person searching for you. Believe this, speak the words of power, and the Creative Mother will turn heaven and earth to bring the two of you together. On the inner plane, that bonding has already occurred, which will make the recognition of each other truly a magical moment. Jan and I know. It happened to us. Permit me to get a bit personal here and tell our story:

I had a casual acquaintance with a young girl who lived down the street from me when I was a teenager. I was a senior in high school at the time, and she was only a freshman, just a kid. Years later, while on leave from the Air Force, my mother gave an open house for me, and during the festivities, a beautiful young woman walked gracefully into view. It was that kid all grown up, and just like in the movies, our eyes met, an electric shock went through me, and I knew I'd never be the same. What I didn't know at that moment was that she was having a similar experience.

Six months later, in June of 1953, Jan Bryant and I were married. Someone once wrote and asked me what made our relationship, after these many years, so ideal. I said, "Her happiness means more to me than my own, and my happiness means more to her than her own. We want the most for each other, and when that kind of attitude and feeling merge as one from both perspectives, you have a bond of love and joy that overshadows everything." I also believe that in any loving relationship there must be reciprocal roles, neither one domineering or submissive. It's that kind of equal partnership in life that makes things work so beautifully.

Before I digressed, we were discussing words of power. I want to introduce one that will be highly significant in the alchemical process. It is **Yes**, with multiple *s*'s following—that is, **Yes***sss*. To explain, I refer to Dr. Douglas M. Baker's book, *The Diary of An Alchemist.* He equates the **s-s-s** sound with the fire of the alchemist, a divine breath that can be radiated through an individual's aura to sustain the form coming forth out of substance. He calls the **s-s-s** a radioactive force, the energy of the universe, with the swan being the symbol for this spiritual fire. He writes:

> Swans and fire—the two are synonymous in the highest expressions of alchemical symbols.[4]
>
> The pronunciation of the letter **S** requires the shaping of the mouth so that a very discreet jet of air is emitted. This is the divine breath, the fire snorted from the nostrils of the dragon, the audio-fiery torrent seen as flame by the devas.[5]

In experimenting with the alchemical process, I attempted to use the hissing sound in the various steps, but found little vibratory response from within. Then one day the inner voice said, "Apply the word **Yes** with the sound following during the unity of spirit and matter." **Yes***ssss!* This word of power was to be used to energize and activate the desired manifestation. I realized then what a vital link it was in the overall process.

Practice sounding the **Yes***ssss*. It will soon become one of your favorite words.

✳✳✳

Chapter Eleven

Perfecting the Masterpiece

*W*e have touched on controlled visualization or active imagination in previous chapters. Now it is time to concentrate fully on the images that we will impress upon the World Mother during the alchemical process.

Ask your Holiness to show you the high vision of the most complete life. Let the ultimate be revealed, not letting the ego limit the full scope of the vision. What do you see? With Spirit as your guide, push the envelope, expand the circle, and reach for the highest and grandest life imaginable. Add the little nuances, the special flavor, the highest tone of harmony—all the beauty and nobility that is rightly yours as God in Expression.

Dr. Joseph Murphy, the inspirational teacher and author, has written:

> When the world says, "It is impossible; it can't be done," the man with disciplined, controlled, and directed imagination says, "It IS done!"
>
> It is just as easy—and far more interesting, captivating, and alluring—for you to imagine yourself to be rich and

successful as it is to dwell on poverty, penury, and failure. If you wish to bring about the realization of your desires or ideals, form a mental picture of fulfillment in your mind; constantly imagine the reality of your desire. In this way, you will actually force it into being.[1]

Dr. Murphy also says:

In the science of imagination, you eliminate all the mental impurities, such as envy, covetousness, fear, worry, and jealousy. You must focus all your attention on your goals and objectives in life and refuse to be swerved from your purpose or aim, which is to lead a rich and happy life. Become mentally absorbed in the reality of your desires, and you will see them take material form in your world.

Your sustained imagination is sufficient to remake your world. Trust the laws of your mind to bring your good to pass, and you will experience all the blessings and riches of life.[2]

Dr. Murphy adds that through the *alchemy of the mind*, we weave the fabric out of which our dreams are clothed. Yes, and our nightmares, too. If our vision is downward, with the focus on scarcity, failure, discord, and illness, that's what we're weaving. What do you want in life? What can you see? How expansively can you envision your personal world?

Through spiritual vision, look at these aspects of your Ideal Life. See the perfect mental pictures in your mind—complete with color, sound, animation, and feeling. See yourself in these five facets of life, and take your time as you relish the drama and excitement of each scene.

1. Your spiritual life. Look at the various activities—the learning, the growing, and the realizations. See yourself so filled with the Light of Spirit that you know without a shadow of a doubt that you are a full and glorious manifestation of the *All*. Feel the Presence, the Life, the Love, the Power. Accept the fact that you are a spiritual being now—not in the future, but *now*, the completeness of God in individual expression.

How do you see yourself as a spiritual being of the universe living on Planet Earth? What are you saying and doing? How are you acting? Are you living with unconditional love and spiritual understanding while maintaining mastery over this world? Look at yourself on the stage of life from the Ideal spiritual perspective.

2. Your service to others as a true success in life. See yourself adding your piece of the puzzle, bringing your individual contribution to the Divine Plan. The Angel of Service and Synthesis once told me in meditation:

> *Find that which offers you the greatest personal satisfaction and develop the skill-in-action to use that proficiency for the general good, not necessarily from a global perspective. All activity goes into the stream of life at the point of individual contribution, yet the stream is universal, so what one person does affects everyone to some degree. You love to write. Someone else may enjoy bringing order into a business and fine-tuning the operations for a higher degree of productivity. Another may wish to paint works of art, creations that enter the waters to reflect greater beauty in the world. Others may teach, sing, sell, repair, or manufacture; it makes little difference so long as the individual is deriving full pleasure*

from a principled activity, for it is in the joy of doing
that the currents are stirred, the ripples reach beyond
time and space, and service is fulfilled.[3]

Use your active imagination now, and see yourself doing your part to make this a better world, providing assistance to others without infringing on their independence, and promoting a sense of cooperation and unity among people. This is true success. Develop the image and hold it firm in mind, remembering:

> *Success is the natural order of the universe,*
> *wholly ordained by God as a force for good to*
> *replace the effects of this world with divine reality—*
> *to transform failure to fulfillment, lack to abundance,*
> *illness to wholeness, and discord to harmony as the*
> *Power moves through us to accomplish and achieve*
> *in accordance with the Law of Being.*[4]

3. Your physical body. Remember that what you see you shall become, so begin to visualize your body exactly as you want it to be. Impregnate Creative Mind only with wholeness, health, and well-being as you see the perfect image of your physical system. See the entire atomic structure in perfect balance, the cells singing songs of joy, every organ in tune with the Great Architect of the body and expressing only the divine activity of life.

In your mental movie, see yourself as active, vital, vigorous, energetic, and playful. Hear yourself saying how wonderful you feel. Listen to others as they say how good you look.

4. Your finances. You are as rich as you can imagine and as wealthy as you can feel, for the universe puts no limits on your financial well-being. But money for money's sake is not the objective. How will you live, what will you have, with an all-sufficiency of funds at your disposal?

First, imagine yourself as totally debt-free, and capture the intense feeling of joy of owing no one anything but love. Ponder this sense of freedom for a moment.

Now feel what it means to have all the money you'll ever need for the rest of your life. How does it feel to be *wealthy*? Put on the mantle of wealth and wear it. There's no pride or pomposity here. You are simply assuming the role that has been yours since the beginning of creation. You are a noble soul, a resident of the kingdom, a divine expression of the Abundance of God. Experience in mind the graciousness, the harmony, and the beauty.

Bring your ideal home into mind. Create the perfect dwelling place in your controlled visualization. Walk around it and look at the beauty, symmetry, and grace. Notice the loveliness of nature surrounding it, the awe-inspiring trees and flowers. Listen to the birds sing. Feel the warmth of the sun. Now walk inside the home, and explore the magnificence of your creation.

I mention the home here because of its importance, symbolically, as your state of consciousness. Valerie Moolman writes in *The Meaning of Your Dreams*:

> A house that is in good condition, with many lovely well-appointed rooms, suggests a dreamer who is healthy and serene. . . . A house that is airy, bright, cheerful, uncluttered and reasonably well organized suggests a dreamer with those same characteristics. . . .[5]

The ideal home impressed upon the Feminine Principle works wonders in both the inner (activities in consciousness) and the outer (the physical manifestation).

Keep expanding your vision and deepening your feelings as you capture the true meaning of living richly and blissfully.

5. Your relationships. See meaningful scenes of harmonious interaction with others—of loving, playing, and being with the perfect mate, the ideal circle of friends, and family members who contribute to your happiness and you to theirs. See yourself as worthy of participating in life with people who are enjoyable, encouraging, harmonious, helpful, and a pleasure to be with. And see yourself adding to the joys of their lives by being a "lifter"—someone people run *to*, rather than *from*.

Create the scenes now of true loving relationships, seeing a variety of activities where the essence of happiness and great joy is shown on the screen of your mind.

Finally, perfect the masterpiece with other scenarios and experiences that would add to your Ideal Life, and put it all in writing. Take each point, and write in your journal what you see . . . what you *want* to see.

I see myself living as I have always dreamed, yet now the dream is a reality, for I have awakened to the vision of truth.

Now we are ready to begin the alchemical process.

✳✳✳

Chapter Twelve

The Alchemical Process

*B*efore you begin the actual process, please make sure that you have:

* carefully read the book up to this chapter and worked with the alchemical exercises.

* met with the 22 angels in an exploratory session. (Chapter 4)

* taken on the energies of Power and Authority and Spiritual Strength and Will. (Chapter 4)

* worked in mind and feelings with the Saturn energy, and practiced *being* Saturn in consciousness as the Light of God, the Angel of the Presence. (Chapter 5)

* followed the cleansing work with forgiveness, denials of limiting appearances, and a healing of the past. (Chapter 6)

✳ completed the ten structuring lessons, including the mother and mother-in-law evaluations. (Chapter 6)

✳ made contact with Isis and asked her cooperation in creating a new life for yourself. (Chapter 7)

✳ worked with the exercises to come into greater alignment with the emanation of the World Mother, Isis unveiled. (Chapter 8)

✳ studied the Hermetic Principles. (Chapter 9)

✳ written in your journal thoughts of truth and words of power that apply specifically to the creation of your Ideal Life, and practiced using the **Yes**ssss sound. (Chapter 10)

✳ perfected your masterpiece by putting into writing what you can see from the highest vision, the grandest life imaginable. (Chapter 11)

Once this is done, you are ready for the alchemical process.

Relax completely now, and take each step in contemplative meditation to familiarize yourself with the process, then repeat it with deep feeling and expanded vision.

Step 1: Know thy self.
My true and Only Self is the omniscient, omnipotent Spirit of God, the Master Mind that constitutes my Reality. I am the Shining Sun of God, and the fullness of the universe flows through me at every moment.
I speak the words of Truth:

*I am the Universal Consciousness of Wholeness
in radiant expression. I am the Shining Sun of
Complete Well-Being.*

*I am the Universal Consciousness of Abundance
individualized and in radiant expression. I am the
Shining Sun of Infinite Supply.*

*I am the Universal Consciousness of Success
individualized and in radiant expression. I am the
Shining Sun of Divine Accomplishment.*

*I am the Universal Consciousness of Right
Relations individualized and in radiant expression.
I am the Shining Sun of Love and Harmony.*

Step 2: Secure the cooperation of the 22 angels.

I recognize these angels within as living Governors of Life, each controlling a Gate, or opening, leading to the phenomenal world—conditioning and determining all outer expression. I understand that they live on the inner planes of consciousness as extensions of my Whole Self. I seek to ensure that they are all in harmony with me and my objectives.

I ask now that the Inner Guide aspect of my Spirit personally escort me into deep inner space to meet with them. I close my eyes and feel the light all around me as I am led through a winding tunnel. I am safe and secure on this inner journey, and my pace quickens as I see radiant lights ahead, each beginning to take on the form and appearance of 22 beings. I look into the eyes of each one and express my love and gratitude.

I step back from the group now and speak these words:

*I have called this meeting with pure intentions
and love in my heart. I am embarking on a dynamic
alchemical process to change my life from a lower*

vibration to the highest ideal, and I need your full cooperation. I ask you to balance your masculine and feminine qualities, to harmonize any conflicting energy patterns brought on by my ego projections, and to work together as a team in full support of the Angel of Success and Fulfillment and the Angel of Union and Receptivity, as these two angels will form mighty links in the manifestation chain. To do this, let us meditate together on love, joy, and peace.

We are the love of God as one. (Silence) *We are the joy of God as one.* (Silence) *We are the peace of God as one.* (Silence) *Our vibrations are now in harmony, and divine order prevails throughout the inner planes of consciousness.*

I now listen for any response from within, for a message from any particular angel. I listen, and I write what I hear.

Step 3: The fusion of the Angel of Power and Authority and the Angel of Spiritual Strength and Will, and the embodiment of the blended energy force.

I now invite the Angels of Power and Authority and Spiritual Strength and Will to come to me and blend their energies. They acknowledge my request, and I see their energy forms coming together as one Being of Light and entering the force field of my consciousness. I now embody this powerful energy, and I speak these words:

My life is ruled only by spiritual power, embodying the fullness of God's Purpose and Power. I am leaving ego domination and rising into the reality of spiritual consciousness.

*I am strong in the mightiness of Spirit, and I am
undaunted. My mind is firmly one-pointed in seeing
only the good. My heart is fearless and knows only
the emotion of victory.*

Step 4: Bond with Saturn, the Light of the Lord.

I now call forth the Archetype of Saturn, the Angel of the
Presence. I see the form and features of this Angel, and as I
look into its eyes with great feeling in my heart, I express my
love and gratitude.

My intention is to merge consciously with this Angel as I
already am in reality. I see myself and the energy literally becoming one. It is the Angel of Light, the light shining from
Spirit-Self. I acknowledge the Source of the light and feel the
radiation upon me as from a giant searchlight, the rays beaming in, around, and through me.

I now speak these words with great feeling:

I am the Angel of Light.
I am the Angel of the Dawn.
I am the Angel of the Presence.
I am Success and Fulfillment.
I am the Law unto my world.

Step 5: Bond with Isis, the Creative Mind.

I turn now to the High Priestess, and as I draw closer to
her, I see the form and appearance of her symbolic representation. I look into her eyes, express my love with deep feelings,
and say to her:

*I have taken on the energy of Saturn, the Angel
of the Presence, as the identity of my personality,*

*and I seek now to bond with you completely in con-
sciousness. My objective is to live as I was created to
live—with beauty, nobility, and harmony, and I know
you can reveal this Ideal Life for me.*

I now feel the bonding taking place. We are one, and in this
oneness, I say to this great Creative Principle:

*From this day forward, I will do my very best to
make sure that the thoughts of discord and disharmony do not reach you.*

*With all my mind and heart, I will protect you
from the negative forces of fear, anger, resentment,
and guilt.*

*I will treat you with the respect of an aspect of
my divinity, and will give you thoughts and feelings
of only the highest order.*

*In turn, I ask that you be responsive to my will-
for-good, which is in harmony with the universal
truth, goodness, and beauty.*

I now listen to her response.

Step 6: Think thoughts of truth; speak words of power.
Use your own thoughts and words, with the following as
reminders:

*The Creative Principle is healing my mind of all
false beliefs and error patterns, and is restoring and
maintaining my body in perfect health.*

*I am a spiritual being with a physical form. That
form is fashioned after the perfect Life Pattern;*

therefore, my body is perfect and is in a state of complete healthfulness.

I live and move and have my being in lavish abundance. I cannot be limited, for I am the law of expansion, increase, and fruition. A magnificent harvest of excess is springing forth at every moment, ready for gathering.

I am the Spirit of Infinite Plenty. I am wealthy because I am the Kingdom of Wealth. I am the Shining Sun of Magnificent Prosperity.

I am enjoying the fullness of unlimited success, for I am in my true place doing what I love and loving what I do for the good of all. I am the Spirit of Accomplishment, the Force of Achievement, and every activity of life reflects the ideals of victory and triumph.

I am the consciousness to do, be, and have.
I am the power to be successful.
I am the energy of success.

My inner Light now draws to me those with whom I can relate in love, peace, and joy. Because it is the principle of right relations in action, my desires are beautifully fulfilled, my needs easily met.

Creative Mind is securing the bond of harmlessness and harmony between me and everyone else in my world, and the activity of divine attraction and right relations is eternally operating in my life.

Step 7: Impress Isis with your mental movie of the Ideal Life, your vision of your perfect personal world in every aspect.

Refer now to your masterpiece in writing, or use your creative imagination to see the ultimate in life, not limiting yourself in any way. Spend several minutes in controlled visualization, knowing that you are impressing your images upon Creative Mind.

Step 8: Speak to the Creative Feminine Principle.

You have been given the vision and the truth, and the units of your energy are now configured into the perfect pattern for manifestation. The Virgin now becomes the Mother to birth and nourish my Ideal Life.

Step 9: See and feel the energy-substance of the Mother-Spirit radiating through the pattern, the blueprint of the Ideal, and out through your throat chakra.

See the radiation going before you as a golden stream of energy, and in that stream, see the unity of Spirit and matter. See-feel the perfect physical body, the lavish abundance of money-in-form, the fulfillment of true success, and the people in your life expressing love and harmony in ideal relationships. See and feel the good, true, and beautiful experiences—the Ideal Life—all within the flowing stream of energy.

Step 10: Say Yes*ssss*.

Meditate on the reality of the complete manifestation of your Ideal Life. And to what you are seeing, say **Yes*ssss***, the hiss of the swan to each form and experience. See your ideal body and **Yes*ssss*** it. Consume it with fire, and release the perfection. Look at the money, the great wealth, and **Yes***ssss* it with fire—energize it! Look at the symbols of your success, and **Yes***ssss* them with activation. Look at your loving and harmonious relationships, and **Yes***ssss* them with fire to support and maintain them.

Step 11: Establish the Law of Attraction through love.

Close the curtain on your mind, turn your attention to your heart center, and feel the magnetic power of love. Turn on the love! Feel it! Let it flow! This activates the Law of Attraction to draw the manifest experiences back to you. Love attracts what love has formed. Spend several minutes in and with the love vibration.

Step 12: Feel the gratitude.

Enter now into an intense and continuous feeling of thankfulness. Praise God from whom all blessings flow! Express deep gratitude to the Mother-Spirit for all the good that has been manifest, and is now coming to you. Love and adore your Holiness with great appreciation.

✳✳✳

Now that you are familiar with the complete process, go through it again and make it natural for you by using your own thoughts, words, and interpretations of the steps. Just make sure that all 12 are covered.

✳✳✳

Chapter Thirteen

The Creative Feminine Principle Does the Work

*I*t is suggested that you work with the alchemical process daily until you have the feeling of *inner* confidence, contentment, and fulfillment. The feeling of HAVE must first be registered within before it can be manifest in the outer. Once this has been achieved, it is time to relax and let the creative power complete the process. You continue to live the Truth—holding to your high vision; thinking only constructive thoughts; feeling only love, joy, and peace in your heart; and seeing everyone as totally fulfilled in life. This is your role as a co-creator.

When you consciously took on the energies of Power and Authority and Spiritual Strength and Will, and then the Saturn energy of Cause, your mind and heart together moved to a higher vibration, a higher frequency in consciousness, overriding the ego and putting you in direct alignment with your Whole Self. Then, in your interaction with the Feminine Principle of Isis-Mother, you impressed the Truth to bring your life up to the Divine Standard where there is no lack of anything good, true, and beautiful.

As the manifestations occur and you see your Ideal Life coming more into view, remember that everything that appears is an effect resulting from Cause. It is your masterpiece of your perfect world design coming forth as an atomic structure that appears as material form or physical experience because your mind "arrests" the energy vibration to enable you to perceive the form and enjoy the experience. The healed body, the money, the creative accomplishment, and the harmonized and loving relationships are all the result of the energy of manifestation, the law of Cause, with all that appears being interpretations of your consciousness.

And with this awareness comes spiritual understanding. You love the forms and experiences now appearing as part of your Ideal Life, but at the same time, you do not depend only on the manifestations to bring you complete joy and peace. You understand that a well body is not your wholeness, money is not your supply, your work is not your security, and relationships do not constitute your support. You know what is. *God.* The Spirit of *All* within is the only source of happiness, and you realize that if you try to find your total bliss in what you have manifested through the alchemical process, you will interrupt the continuing flow of *complete* fulfillment on both the inner and outer planes.

For example, through the alchemical process, three of my nonfiction manuscripts, including this one, were quickly accepted by a publisher. I was not looking at the publishing of these books as the *source* of my joy, but rather as the fruits of my joy-filled days of writing, as books that should be available to people as part of the service mode of my ideal vision—and the contracts were soon on their way. However, the process produced absolutely no activity on the novels I had written.

While meditating on this, it came to me that I was relying on the sale of my fictional works as the source of my prosperity, my real accomplishment in life, my true happiness. By focusing strictly on these effects for personal satisfaction, I had deserted the true Source, and no home could be found for the novels. All doors seemed closed. It was only after I worked the process again, this time thinking of the novels only as delightful exercises in creativity that contributed to my fulfillment simply in the writing, did I have a breakthrough. I received a call from a production company in Los Angeles wanting an option on a love story I had written. The title of the manuscript is *To Love Again*, and they wanted to consider it for a major motion picture. And I'm confident now that the publishing of all of my novels will soon be on the horizon.

Do you understand the significance of this? When I ceased focusing on the manifest effects as the *source* of my prosperity, my success, and my happiness, the door was opened. Spirit is our only source of joy and delight. Let's keep that truth etched deeply in consciousness.

The whole purpose of the alchemical process is to change our thinking and feeling natures, move up to a higher frequency in consciousness, and see what we *want* in life, rather than what we do not want. It is clearing the channels for creative mind and getting us back into the natural order of the universe, where we see the infinite possibilities of life more abundantly. We clean up the past, remove our ego projections on others, begin to think and feel rightly, and use our active imagination in only the most productive way. This impresses the Mother Principle within to express constructively, and we see more of heaven appearing on earth. But these appearances, these more fulfilling experiences, are not to be considered the source of our love, joy, peace, harmony, and contentment. Yes, we enjoy the manifestations, but we do not give them the power to rule our lives.

God is the only Source of my happiness. This master thought and feeling will impregnate the Feminine Power and bring forth more of the manifest kingdom with its glorious experiences than we could have possibly imagined. The reason is that we have moved from *depending* on effects, to *enjoying* them, which clears the channel for even more good. We work from the highest standpoint in thought, word, and vision while depending totally on the *All* of Being for everything that means anything in life. This is co-creation—where we work to do our part, then place our complete reliance on Divine Grace, the Love of God, to do the rest. One without the other does not bring lasting results. It must be a cooperative effort.

Kathryn, from Michigan, attended our Alchemy School, and within days of returning home, she wrote that the color of her teeth beneath the veneers had changed from a dull yellow to a bright and beautiful white. She had been visualizing a young body, and in her e-mail message, she said, "My teeth became young!"

In her second communication nearly a month later, she wrote that she had begun to feel impatient:

I was expecting everything to manifest that moment, and if it didn't, I felt that I had to work harder. What I realized was that I was not doing the work—God was. My job was to be in the Divine flow. I feel empowered to create and accept what I want in life, then trust God's Grace to bring it forth. This is the most powerful lesson for me. I create with the alchemy process, then trust God's Grace. I let the Grace do the work.

She went on to say what had happened since this realization:

I've been extremely healthy. I feel so good and have so much energy and my body is toning up quickly. And I have an abundance of money—plenty to do whatever I want to do.

Now let's read about other amazing results from the alchemical process, remembering that what others have done, you can do as well. The universe is for *you*, and the only limitations are those that are self-imposed. Free yourself this day, and move toward the fulfillment of your dreams.

✳✳✳

Chapter Fourteen

More Fruits of the Harvest

Sharon, from Texas, kept a journal following the Alchemy School and shared it with us. A few excerpts are as follows.

I feel invigorated and joyous as I walk the body with ease, flexibility, vibrant health, well-being, and strength. It is exhilarating to exercise with the awareness of body and spirit as one.

I am truly making the love connection with all people with whom I interact. No matter what the physical, emotional, or mental state they are in, I can choose to hold the truth and beauty of their higher self in mind and connect with them on that level. The results are amazing.

I find myself experiencing more grace, confidence, and a sense of presence in my life. It comes from knowing more who I am and acknowledging the truth in others. I am more at ease with strangers and find myself in conversations I would never have had before. People seem more comfortable with me, and I feel more comfortable with them and myself. I am experiencing a wonderful exchange of energies. I don't know how to explain what is going on except to say I feel more *at-one-ment* with the universe. Then an insight came: It is not I, but God expressing through me. I need only let it happen and accept His loving bounty.

Through the practice of alchemy, I now realize the truth of who I am. My consciousness is more open and receptive to this truth, and my body can and does manifest the wholeness and vibrating health of the higher self. Spirit and body in unity!

Jean, of Arkansas, wrote the following after attending the Alchemy School:

It's such a joy to be an awakening alchemist. I feel that the power of alchemy is so great that only a few are needed to create and maintain the balance needed for the peace process to develop on earth.

Again, the reference to the unity of spirit and "this world."

Incidentally, Jean's objective at the school was to create understanding within a family member and assist the person in dealing with a particular relationship. Not only was she highly successful, but there was an interesting side effect. She began finding money wherever she went, whether a walk down the street or while taking a stroll through the park—and not only coins, but bills of various denominations. And in a recent communication, she joyfully reported that two weeks after attending the Alchemy School, the coins she had collected at home began *multiplying*—more than ten times the original amount, according to her calculations.

While working on this chapter, I heard from David, in Texas, also a participant at the school. He told about finding his soulmate through the alchemical process, and I asked him to relate the experience for this chapter. He wrote:

In June of 1998, I basically told God that either I be sent the ideal mate or I was prepared to live alone the rest of my life. I truly wanted to experience a soul-connected, heart-centered relationship. As soon as I made this proclamation to God, a bubble went up around me. What I mean is that I could not get a date. Women would go the opposite direction when I approached them. It was if I had the plague, and considering I have had no problem in meeting new women, I found myself bothered by all of this at first. Then it became funny because I also realized that I was being protected and prepared for my life partner coming in.

In 1999, I had decided to take all of the workshops that the Quartus Foundation was going to conduct that year. The first one was in March of 1999, the Alchemy School where John and Jan were going to talk about certain techniques to bring things we desire into our lives. I thought, *What a great opportunity to bring a soulmate in.* During one of the sessions, we were asked to draw a symbol of what we wanted in life and to put it into the energy stream that had been painted on paper and tacked to the wall. I sat up the night before trying to decide what symbol I would use for bringing my soulmate in. After some thought, I drew a big pair of red lips. The lips represented the desired relationship and all the wonderful sensuous and passionate aspects that a true relationship can offer, and I put the lips in the energy stream. Then we used the alchemical process.

Afterwards, I looked around, wondering if my soulmate might be one of my classmates, but most people I knew, and everyone else was from out of state—and I didn't want a long-distance relationship. Between the March workshop and June, I was becoming disappointed that no one was surfacing, but I kept working the alchemical process. Soon it was time for the June workshop on Prophecy and Pragmatism, and when I arrived, I knew almost everyone, and of course, there were those from out of state. This workshop was obviously not where it was going to happen.

We were given some free time, and one evening I had the opportunity to be with five or six women, telling stories and having a good time. One of the ladies was Susan from Michigan, who had attended the Alchemy School. As I heard her talk about where she grew up and how she had been exposed to spirituality at an early stage, I found myself being attracted to her. Yet, I said nothing because I thought she was married, and she lived 1,300 miles away in Michigan. After listening to her stories, I realized she was not married.

At the end of the workshop, Susan was the last person I gave a hug to, and when we embraced, something happened. I felt this "click." I was a little stunned and said nothing to Susan about it. Driving home that afternoon, I could feel my heart opening up, but my mind was saying: *She lives in Michigan and you know nothing about her.*

I sent Susan an e-mail that following Monday to see how her trip back home went. I heard back from her, and we began sending e-mails back and forth, and then talking by telephone. She told me that at the March Alchemy School she had put the sun, moon, and stars on the wall as her symbol for bringing a soul-connected relationship into her life. In a few short days, Susan and I realized that what we had asked for had manifested. We had found one another. I traveled to Michigan a few weeks later and spent

11 days with her, and it was like being in heaven. We are now engaged to be married. I had found my soulmate. If anyone has any doubts that soulmates do not exist, then I am here to tell you that they do.

David's experience wasn't an isolated instance of finding the right partner. Another participant at the school, Dori from the Northeast, chose complete fulfillment in life, including the ideal relationship. That was in March 1999. I spoke with her less than six months later, and she announced that she was getting married on September 1999, to a man who "came into her life" shortly after the school.

Eileen, from California, wrote that not only did she experience positive effects from the process, but so did those around her:

> I have noticed changes for my family and friends. My daughter has a new position that shows promise for advancement for her, and another friend sold her house. I end all meditations with the statement, "What I accept for myself, I accept for all others on the face of the planet and beyond." Divine Order and Right Action are truly at work, and life is wonderful.

Elisha, in New Mexico, attended our follow-up Intensive on Prophecy, where we used the alchemical process to develop our own self-fulfilling prophecies. She later wrote:

> On my return home, I took my time going through the mail. A letter from my bank, which I thought to be a mere statement, I opened last—only to discover that the money in my bank account had suddenly expanded by *three* zeros. Can you believe it? I now can, Yes*ssss!*

In other letters from the new alchemists, we were told that following the school, healings in mind and body took place, a loan to a friend was paid back after two years, greater creativity was expressed, and an expanded circle of friends was manifest. Above all, according to many of the participants, there was a deeper realization of their Divine Nature and a new understanding of the universal creative process.

This showed me that dynamic alchemy is not only a way to realize a full expression of life, but is also a path to the higher frequencies of our Holiness. It's like having our cake and eating it too. While the focus initially may be to bring forth a healthier body, more money, a better job, or more loving relationships, what we realize in the process of manifesting our dreams is that we are so much more than we thought we were.

By opening our minds and hearts, we begin to understand the Truth of Being—that we are here to enjoy wholeness, abundance, success, and harmony as part of the natural order of life. *That's the way it's supposed to be!* We have it all and we have it now, and "time" is an element only in our minds; it is not required for divine expression. With that understanding, we establish our Perfect World in consciousness, and place our full dependence on the emanating energy to bring it all into visible form and experience.

In the process, we begin to live in the all-inclusive Now, and that's when *time* is no longer a factor in the manifestation of the Ideal Life. Detach yourself from the time equation, and realize that you do not have to wait for the wonders and blessings of God to show forth in every area of your life. They are here now, waiting for eyes to see.

✳✳✳

Before they call, I will answer.
Behold, I make all things new.

✳✳✳

Endnotes

Introduction

1. *A Course In Miracles*, vol. 1, *Text* (Tiburon, Ca.: Foundation for Inner Peace, 1975), p. 27.

2. Kenneth Wapnick, *Forgiveness and Jesus* (Roscoe, NY: Foundation for *A Course In Miracles,* 1983), p. 77.

3. *The Beacon* (India: World Council of Sri Sathya Sai Organisations, 1985), p. 11.

Chapter One: Dynamic Alchemy

1. Manly P. Hall, *The Secret Teachings of All Ages* (Los Angeles: Philosophical Research Society, 1977), p. CLIII.

2. Three Initiates, *The Kybalion—Hermetic Philosophy* (Chicago: The Yogi Publication Society, 1912), p. 22.

3. Ibid., p. 29.

4. Barbara G. Walker, *The Women's Encyclopedia of Myths and Secrets* (Edison, NJ: Castle Books, 1996), p. 18.

Chapter Two: See the Ultimate in Life

1. W. Frederic Keeler, edited by Alma M. Morse, *Solving the*

Problem of Supply (Oakland, Ca.: Lakeside Temple of Practical Christianity, 1971), pp. 5–6.

2. Manly P. Hall, *The Secret Teachings of All Ages* (Los Angeles: Philosophical Research Society, 1977), p. LXXX.

Chapter Three: The Alchemical Trinity

1. John Randolph Price, *The Jesus Code* (Carlsbad, Ca.: Hay House, Inc., 2000), p. 8.

Chapter Four: The Spiritual Forces

1. John Randolph Price, *The Angels Within Us* (New York: Fawcett Columbine/Ballantine, 1993), pp. 9–10.

Chapter Five: Saturn: The Penetrating Law

1. John Randolph Price, *The Angels Within Us* (New York: Fawcett Columbine/Ballantine, 1993), p. 282.

2. Alice A. Bailey, *Esoteric Astrology* (New York: Lucis, 1951), p. 168.

3. Louis Pauwels & Jacques Bergier, *The Morning of the Magicians* (New York: Stein and Day, 1983), p. 89.

4. John Randolph Price, *The Angels Within Us* (New York: Fawcett Columbine/Ballantine, 1993), p. 284.

5. Edwin C. Steinbrecher, *The Inner Guide Meditation* (York Beach, Mn.: Samuel Weiser, Inc., 1988), p. 240.

6. Dr. Paul Foster Case, *Highlights of the Tarot* (Los Angeles: Builders of the Adytum, Ltd. Publishers, 1931), p. 34.

7. Isabel M. Hickey, *Astrology A Cosmic Science* (Sebastopol, Ca.: CRCS Publications, 1992), p. 34.

8. Ibid., p. 41.

9. Ibid., p. 49.

10. *Metaphysical Bible Dictionary* (Unity Village, Mo.: Unity School of Christianity, 1931), p. 567.

11. Ibid., Addenda, p. III.

12. Ibid., Addenda, p. II.

Chapter Six: Structuring Your Life with Saturn

1. John Jocelyn, *Meditations on the Signs of the Zodiac* (San Francisco: Harper & Row, Publishers, 1970), p. 214.

2. John Randolph Price, *The Superbeings* (mass-market edition, New York: Fawcett Crest, Ballantine Books, 1988; trade edition: Carlsbad, Ca.: Hay House, Inc., 1997), pp. 78–79.

3. Catherine Ponder, *The Dynamic Laws of Prayer* (Marina Del Ray, Ca.: DeVorss & Company, 1987), pp. 80–81.

4. Robert Hand, *Planets in Transit* (Atglen, Pa.: Whitford Press, 1976), p. 317.

5. Isabel M. Hickey, *Astrology A Cosmic Science* (Sebastopol, Ca.: CRCS Publications, 1992), p. 35.

6. Ibid., p. 33.

7. Ibid., p. 33.

8. Robert Hand, *Planets in Transit* (Atglen, Pa.: Whitford Press, 1976), p. 317.

9. Isabel M. Hickey, *Astrology A Cosmic Science* (Sebastopol, Ca.: CRCS Publications, 1992), p. 33.

10. Alice A. Bailey, *Esoteric Healing* (New York: Lucis, 1953), p. 5.

11. Alice A. Bailey, *The Externalisation of the Hierarchy* (New York: Lucis, 1958), p. 335.

12. Manly P. Hall, *The Secret Teachings of All Ages* (Los Angeles: Philosophical Research Society, 1977), p. CCII.

13. Newton Dillaway, ed., *The Gospel of Emerson* (Wakefield, Ma.: The Montrose Press, 1949), p. 73.

Chapter Seven: Veiled Isis: The Receptive Sheath

1. Manly P. Hall, *The Secret Teachings of All Ages* (Los Angeles: Philosophical Research Society, 1977), p. XLV.

2. Ibid., p. XLVI.

3. Barbara G. Walker, *The Women's Encyclopedia of Myths and Secrets* (Edison, NJ: Castle Books, 1997), p. 345.

4. Isabel M. Hickey, *Astrology A Cosmic Science*

(Sebastopol, Ca.: CRCS Publications, 1992), p. 38.

5. Dr. Paul Foster Case, *Highlights of Tarot* (Los Angeles: Builders of the Adytum, Ltd. Publishers, 1931), p. 19.

6. Alfred Douglas, *The Tarot* (New York: Viking Penguin Inc., 1972), p. 55.

7. Edwin C. Steinbrecher, *The Inner Guide Meditation* (York Beach, Mn.: Samuel Weiser, Inc., 1988), p. 240.

8. Three Initiates, *The Kybalion—Hermetic Philosophy* (Chicago: The Yogi Publication Society, 1912), p. 193.

9. Ibid., p. 202.

10. Alice A. Bailey, *Telepathy* (New York: Lucis, 1950), p. 47.

11. Ibid., p. 54.

Chapter Eight: Isis Unveiled: The Creative Power

1. Alfred Douglas, *The Tarot* (New York: Viking Penguin Inc., 1972), p. 58.

2. Vitvan, *The Natural Order Process*, vol. I (Baker, Nv.: School of the Natural Order, Inc., 1968), p. 14.

3. Ibid., p. 43.

4. Ibid., p. 7.

5. Alice A. Bailey, *Esoteric Astrology* (New York: Lucis, 1951), p. 246.

6. W. Frederic Keeler, edited by Alma M. Morse, *Solving the Problem of Supply* (Oakland, Ca.: Lakeside Temple of Practical Christianity, 1971), pp. 5–6.

Chapter Nine: Achieving Right Understanding

1. Three Initiates, *The Kybalion—Hermetic Philosophy* (Chicago: The Yogi Publication Society, 1912), p. 28.

2. Charles F. Haanel, *The Master Key* (Marple, Cheshire, England: Psychological Publishing Co. Ltd., 1976), pp. 117–118.

3. Barbara G. Walker, *The Women's Encyclopedia of Myths and Secrets* (Edison, NJ: Castle Books, 1996), p. 183.

4. Vitvan, *The Natural Order Process*, vol. I, (Baker, Nv.: School of the Natural Order, Inc., 1968), p. 45.

Chapter Ten: Thoughts of Truth, Words of Power

1. Charles F. Haanel, *The Master Key* (Marple, Cheshire, England: Psychological Publishing Co. Ltd., 1976), pp. 289–290.

2. John Randolph Price, *The Angels Within Us* (New York: Fawcett Columbine/Ballantine, 1993), pp. 289–290.

3. John Randolph Price, *Living a Life of Joy* (New York: Fawcett Columbine/Ballantine, 1997), p. 105.

4. Douglas Baker, *The Diary of An Alchemist* (Potters Bar, England: The College of Spiritual Enlightenment and Esoteric Knowledge, 1977), p. 11.

5. Ibid., p. 10.

Chapter Eleven: Perfecting the Masterpiece

1. Joseph Murphy, *Your Infinite Power To Be Rich* (West Nyack, NY: Parker Publishing Company, Inc., 1966), pp. 143–144.

2. Ibid., pp. 150–151.

3. John Randolph Price, *The Angels Within Us* (New York: Fawcett Columbine/Ballantine, 1993), p. 241.

4. Ibid., p. 279.

5. Valerie Moolman, *The Meaning of Your Dreams* (New York: Castle Books, 1969), p. 82.

About the Author

John Randolph Price is a bestselling author and chairman of The Quartus Foundation for Spiritual Research, Inc. He and his wife, Jan, were the originators of "World Healing Day"— a global mind-link for peace that began at noon Greenwich time on December 31, 1986, with over 500 million participants. It has continued to be a yearly event in more than 100 countries.

For information about workshops, the annual Mystery School conducted by the Prices, and their monthly publications, please contact:

The Quartus Foundation
P.O. Box 1768
Boerne, TX 78006

Phone: **(830) 249-3985**
Fax: **(830) 249-3318**
E-mail: **quartus@texas.net**

Please visit the Quartus Website at: **quartus.org**

✳✳✳

Other Hay House Titles of Related Interest

Healing with the Angels
How the Angels Can Assist You in Every Area of Your Life,
by Doreen Virtue, Ph.D.

Holy Spirit
The Boundless Energy of God,
by Ron Roth, Ph.D.

Journeys with a Brother: Japan to India
Bartholomew and the Dalai Lama in the Himalayas,
by Bartholomew

Pathways to the Soul
101 Ways to Open Your Heart,
by Carlos Warter, M.D., Ph.D.

Sixth Sense
Including the Secrets of the Etheric Subtle Body,
by Stuart Wilde

7 Paths to God
The Ways of the Mystic,
by Joan Borysenko, Ph.D.

✳✳✳

(All of the books above can be ordered through
your local bookstore, or by calling Hay House at
the numbers on the last page.)

Notes

Notes

Notes

Notes

Notes

Notes

Notes

Notes

We hope you enjoyed this Hay House book. If you would like
to receive a free catalog featuring additional Hay House books
and products, or if you would like information about
the Hay Foundation, please contact:

Hay House, Inc.
P.O. Box 5100
Carlsbad, CA 92018-5100
(760) 431-7695 or **(800) 654-5126**
(760) 431-6948 (fax) or **(800) 650-5115 (fax)**
www.hayhouse.com

Published and distributed in Australia by:
Hay House Australia Pty. Ltd. • 18/36 Ralph St. • Alexandria
NSW 2015 • *Phone:* 612-9669-4299 • *Fax:* 612-9669-4144
www.hayhouse.com.au

Published and distributed in the United Kingdom by:
Hay House UK, Ltd. • Unit 62, Canalot Studios • 222 Kensal
Rd., London W10 5BN • *Phone:* 44-20-8962-1230
Fax: 44-20-8962-1239 • www.hayhouse.co.uk

Published and distributed in the Republic of South Africa by:
Hay House SA (Pty), Ltd., P.O. Box 990, Witkoppen 2068
Phone/Fax: 2711-7012233 • orders@psdprom.co.za

Distributed in Canada by:
Raincoast • 9050 Shaughnessy St., Vancouver, B.C. V6P 6E5
Phone: (604) 323-7100 • *Fax:* (604) 323-2600

❋ ❋ ❋

Sign up via the Hay House USA Website to receive the
Hay House online newsletter and stay informed about what's
going on with your favorite authors. You'll receive bimonthly
announcements about: Discounts and Offers, Special Events,
Product Highlights, Free Excerpts, Giveaways, and more!
www.hayhouse.com

CPSIA information can be obtained
at www.ICGtesting.com
Printed in the USA
BVHW082232201120
593597BV00002B/149